A MISSIONARY IN NEW GUINEA . . .
A NASA SATELLITE TRACKING CHIEF . . .

An Iowa schoolteacher, an Oklahoma truck driver, a Portuguese kindergarten teacher, a Russian physicist, a Virginia minister, a Seattle physician, an American Air Force captain, more than 50 pilots for commercial air lines—

ALL HAVE SEEN, REPORTED, DESCRIBED UFO'S!

The Air Force tells the public that Flying Saucers are "Natural Phenomena"—that they are only sun spots, or even *imagination!* But evidence contradictory to that easy theory mounts daily as new UFO sightings occur. The answer may still be just beyond reach—but the facts themselves will amaze you!

STRANGERS
FROM
THE SKIES

Brad Steiger

AWARD BOOKS   •   NEW YORK

AWARD BOOKS
First printing 1966

AWARD BOOKS are published by
Universal Publishing and Distributing Corporation
800 Second Avenue, New York, New York 10017

Manufactured in the United States of America

TABLE OF CONTENTS

1.

The Saucers and the "Robots" That Terrorized an Argentine Ranch

"Senor Moreno! Senor Moreno, wake up!"

Antonio Moreno rolled over and blinked into the darkness until his eyes reluctantly made out the form of his ranch hand standing in the doorway of the bedroom.

"What is it?" Moreno mumbled. "What's wrong?"

It was 9:30 P.M. on the evening of October 21, 1963, and seventy-two-year-old Antonio Moreno and his sixty-three-year-old wife, Teresa, had gone to bed early. Neither of them was pleased to have his sleep interrupted by an excitable young employee who was probably upset over some matter that could easily have waited until morning.

"There seems to have been an accident on the railroad tracks," the young man said.

"An accident?" Senora Moreno questioned, wrapping a housecoat around her nightgown. "But I am a very light sleeper. The railroad tracks are only a half mile away. I would surely have heard the noise if there had been an accident."

"But there is a very strange light on the tracks, and men are working at something," the young man protested. "See for yourself. You should be able to see the light from your bedroom window."

The Morenos did as their nervous employee requested and were surprised to see a brilliant light floating above a number of men, who seemed to be inspecting the railroad tracks.

"What a bright light," Senor Moreno said, narrowing

7

her eyes as if she were looking into an arc light. "What are those men doing, Antonio?"

"It is indeed peculiar," Moreno frowned. "Why would anyone be inspecting the railroad tracks at this time of night?" Moreno's ranch was near Tranca, in Cordoba province, Argentina. The area was not so isolated that railroad crews needed to put in overtime to perform maintenance duties.

"That great light moved!" the employee shouted. "It moved at least twenty feet down the track."

Moreno put a forefinger to his lips. "Don't shout," he admonished the young man. "Senora Moreno's sister and her children are asleep in the next room. There is no need to awaken them for such a silly reason. The light is obviously on some elevated railroad flatcar."

"My curiosity is aroused," Senora Moreno said, reaching for the flashlight which she kept beside her bed. "I'm going to walk down the tracks and see what those men are doing."

Moreno started to protest, then shrugged his shoulders. He knew that it was useless to argue with his wife once she had decided upon a particular course of action.

Senora Moreno did not get very far. At the sound of the closing screendoor, the men at the tracks were seen to suddenly direct their attention toward the ranch house. Almost at once, a disc-shaped object, about 25 feet in diameter, swooped down on Senora Moreno. The startled woman retreated into the ranch house, and the entire household, alerted by her screams, watched in terror as the glowing disc hovered at about tree-top level and began to direct a beam of white light at the house.

Senora Moreno gasped in surprise and horror, and her body trembled with a "tingling sensation" when the beam of light entered a window and struck her. One of her sister's children woke with a scream as the beam moved over his body.

"We are being invaded by monsters from outer space!" the young ranch hand cried.

Senora Moreno quieted him. "Help my sister move her

children to places where the light can't strike them. We must be quiet."

Peeping out through a window, Antonio Moreno was horrified to see four other saucers glide up to join the disc that was shooting the strange beams of light at their house. Only one of the new arrivals participated in the attack, however. The other three seemed contented to hover in the air about 210 feet away. Each of the objects was identical with the others—about 25 feet in diameter with a row of windowlike openings, brightly lit, running up the middle.

Members of the besieged household took refuge behind furniture and avoided the windows. Whenever anyone attempted to move, a beam of the "tingling" light would send him scurrying for cover.

"What do the things want with us?" Moreno asked no one in particular. "Why must they do this to us? And what are those shiny suits doing to the railroad tracks?"

Senora Moreno managed another peek out of a window and saw that one of the discs had begun to project a reddish-violet beam while the other maintained the white shafts of light. "The house then became like an oven," the Morenos later told a correspondent for the *Clarim* at Tranca, Argentina.

"They are trying to drive us out!" Senora Moreno's sister began to wail hysterically. "They are trying to smoke us out of our home as if we were animals!"

"Well, we shall not be budged," Senora Moreno announced with determination.

For forty minutes, the beleaguered ranch house withstood the rising temperature engendered by the mysterious hovering saucers. At last, the ranch hand noticed that the "men" at the railroad track had begun to board the disc that had provided them with light for their inspection tour. Within seconds, the terrible beams of light were extinguished, and the discs that had surrounded the ranch house began to move away.

At the moment of the discs' departure, the Morenos' three watch dogs began to raise a terrible fuss, howling, barking, and snarling. "Where were the dogs before?" Moreno puzzled. "It was as if they were stunned."

The entire Moreno household were still "stunned" when correspondents from newspapers arrived to interview them. They told the newsmen that a "thick mist-like smoke, which smelled like sulphur, hung over the trees for several minutes after the departure of the strange aircraft."

The reporter for *Clarim* informed his readers that the smell of sulphur had still permeated the ranch house when he had conducted his interview two days later. The October 24, 1963 issues of both the Rio de Janeiro *Tribuna Da Imprensa* and the Buenos Aires *La Nacion* carried extensive accounts of the hour of terror endured by the Moreno household.

Although the tale of hovering saucers, that directed alternating "tingling" and suffocating beams of light, seems to smack more of fantastic fiction than of reality, the Morenos' story was not without corroborating testimonies and other eyewitness accounts, that tend to make the whole incident rather uncomfortable to contemplate.

A Senor Francisco Tropuano told a correspondent for the France-Press wire service that he had been only a mile away from the Moreno ranch when, at about 10:20, he saw six discs traveling across the sky in close formation. Although he knew nothing of the terrible hour that the Morenos had suffered until he read of it in the papers, Senor Tropuana had discussed his independent sighting quite freely with his friends and neighbors.

Two days before the Morenos' besiegement had been publicized, a truckdriver's encounter with the "tingling" rays of light had been reported in the Monte Maix, Argentina *El Diario* and the *O Jornal* of Rio de Janeiro, Brazil.

Eugenio Douglas, a commercial truckdriver, told correspondents that, on the evening of October 18th, on the highway approaching Monte Maix, his entire truck had become enveloped by a brilliant white light. Senor Douglas had only a few moments to speculate about the source of the light when his entire body began to tingle like "the peculiar sensation one gets when his foot goes to sleep."

Douglas lost control of his truck and drove it into a ditch. The beam seemed to "shut itself off" and the truckdriver, upon clearing his head, saw that the brilliant light had come from a glowing disc, about 25 feet in diameter, which blocked the highway. As he blinked unbelieving eyes, he was approached by "three indescribable beings" which he could only compare to "shiny metal robots."

The terrified truckdriver vaulted from the cab of his vehicle, fired four revolver shots at the approaching monsters and began to run wildly across the open fields. When he at last stopped to catch his breath and look over his shoulder, he saw that the "indescribable beings" had boarded the disc. He was soon to learn that the "robots" had not taken kindly to being fired upon.

After the disc had become airborne, the luminous flying object made several passes over the head of the desperately running truckdriver.

"Each time the disc swooped down on me," Douglas told newsmen, "I felt a wave of terrible, suffocating heat and that prickling sensation."

Eugenio Douglas ran the entire distance to Monte Maix. When he arrived at police headquarters, he was in a near-hysterical condition. As painful evidence to support his incredible tale, his body bore several welt-like burns, which the medical examiner had to admit were "strange and unlike any that I have ever seen." *Accion* reporters from Agrega, Argentina published an interview with the doctor in which the physician conceded that he could "offer no explanation for the burns."

Saucers have often been sighted along railroad tracks, and, recently, theorists have wondered if the discs and their crews might not be more interested in the high-power lines that follow the tracks rather than in the tracks themselves. In the Exeter, New Hampshire sightings in September of 1965 the UFO's were most often reported to be hovering above highpower lines. The 25-foot diameter of the saucers is commonly reported by those who have seen the flying discs. And as subsequent cases will reveal, the sighting of "robots" or "men in shiny suits" is by no means limited to the Pampas. Nor, regrettably, is the "tingling" beam of light which the discs often direct at men, livestock, and machinery.

2.

The Monsters that Came in a Saucer

"It looked worse than Frankenstein," was the way Mrs. Kathleen May described the alien being that she and seven other Flatwoods, West Virginia residents had seen on September 12, 1952.

Mrs. May had had her attention called to the saucer by a group of excited children, including her sons, Eddie, 13, and Fred, 12. The children had been at a nearby playground with Gene Lemon, Neil Nunley, Ronnie Shaver, and Tommy Hyer when they had spotted a "saucer spouting an exhaust that looked like balls of red fire." According to the boys, the saucer had landed on a hilltop above the May house.

"I told them that it was just their imaginations," Mrs. May told reporters, "but the boys kept insisting that they had seen a flying saucer land behind the hill."

Gene Lemon, a husky seventeen-year-old, had found a flashlight and said that he was going to investigate. At the urging of her children, Mrs. May agreed to accompany the teenager, and the small party of West Virginians set out into the night.

"Up on the hill, I could see a reddish glow," said Mrs. May. "I changed my mind about it all being their imaginations, and I was glad that Gene was in the lead."

After about half an hour of tramping through the brush that covered the narrow uphill trail, Gene Lemon's courage left him in a long scream of terror, the intrepid band of saucer-hunters fled in panic from the sight that Lemon's flashlight had illuminated.

When Lemon had flashed the beam on the glowing green spots, he had thought them to be the eyes of an

13

animal. Instead, the flash had spotlighted an immense, man-like figure with a blood-red face and greenish eyes that blinked out from a pointed hood. Behind the monster was "a glowing ball of fire as big as a house" that grew dimmer and brighter at intervals.

Later, Mrs. May described the monster as having "terrible claws." Some of the children, however, had not noticed any arms at all. Most agreed that the being had worn dark clothing, and fourteen-year-old Neil Nunley specified the color to be a "dark green." Estimates of the creature's height ranged from seven feet to ten feet. The party was in definite agreement about one characteristic of the alien, however, and that was the sickening odor which it seemed to emit. Mrs. May told reporters that it was "like sulphur," but really unlike anything that she had ever encountered.

A. Lee Stewart, Jr., of the *Braxton* (West Virginia) *Democrat,* arrived on the scene moments ahead of Sheriff Robert Carr. Although most of the party were too frightened to speak coherently and some were receiving first aid for cuts and bruises received in their pell-mell flight down the hill, the newsman persuaded Lemon to accompany him to the spot where they had seen the being.

Stewart saw no sign of the giant space traveler or of the pulsating red globe of light, but he was able to inhale enough of the strange odor to declare it "sickening and irritating." He later wrote that he had developed a familiarity with a wide variety of gases while serving in the Air Force, but he had never been confronted by any gas with a similar odor.

Each of the party later testified that the monster had been moving toward them, but they also agreed that this might have been due to the fact that they were between the creature and the large, globular object that evidently served as its spacecraft.

Neil Nunley said the alien "didn't really walk. It just moved. It moved evenly: it didn't jump."

On the evening of August 21, 1955, aliens allegedly made the backwoods jump again when they visited Kelly-Hopkinsville, Kentucky. The landing and the subsequent sighting of two to five aliens was witnessed by eight adults and three children. The Air Force, local authorities, the police, and area newspapers conducted an extensive and well-documented investigation of the incident. The adults involved were rather staid, reserved people hardly likely to have invented the entire adventure simply for the sake of sensational publicity. Some even went so far as to leave town when the curiosity seekers and cultists began to arrive, and they remained consistently reluctant to speak about the ordeal with Air Force officials and other investigators.

It was a Sunday evening, and company had gathered at Gaither McGehe's farm, which was currently being rented by the Sutton family. Teen-aged Billy Ray Sutton had left the farmhouse to get a drink from the well. As he drank the cool refreshing water from a chipped cup, he was startled to see a large bright object land about a city block away from the farmhouse.

Billy Ray's announcement of the strange arrival was met with a pronounced lack of response. The family's interest was considerably heightened, however, when, according to several reports, they saw "little men, less than four feet tall with long arms and a large, round head" approaching the farmhouse.

Preserved in Air Force files are drawings that the witnesses made for the investigators. The Suttons testified that the creature's eyes had a yellow glow. The orbs were extremely large and seemed very sensitive to light. It was the outside lights of the farmhouse that seemed to prevent the creature from advancing into the home rather than the bullets from the farmers' rifles, which were fired in great abundance.

"Bullets just seemed to bounce off their nickel-plated armor," said one of the witnesses.

Although the farmers made several direct hits on the aliens, they seemed to "pop right up again and disappear into the darkness, away from the light."

A man named Taylor told investigators: "I knocked one of them off a barrel with my .22. I heard the bullet hit the critter and ricochet off. The little man floated to the ground and rolled up like a ball. I used up four boxes of shells on the little men."

Sutton blasted one of them point-blank with his shotgun, the alien simply somersaulted and rolled off into the darkness.

As with the monster at Flatlands, West Virginia, the witnesses claimed that the aliens did not walk but "seemed to float" toward them.

The farmers battled the seemingly invulnerable creatures for nearly four hours before they drove in panic to the Hopkinsville police station for reinforcements. Chief Greenwell was convinced by the hysteria of the three children and the obvious fright of the eight adults that they had definitely been battling something out on that farm. And everyone knew that the Suttons "weren't a drinking family."

Led by Chief Greenwell, more than a dozen state, county, and city police officers arrived to investigate and, if need arose, to do battle with the little supermen. On the way to the farm, the officers noticed a "strange shower of meteors that came from the direction of the Sutton farmhouse." One officer testified later that the meteors had made a "swishing sound" as they had passed overhead.

The investigators found no trace of a space ship or the little men, but they found "several peculiar signs and indications" that something extremely strange had taken place that evening on the Sutton's farm. Whatever had invaded the Suttons on that Sunday night in August, the bullet holes in the walls bore mute testimony that the farmers had deemed the creatures real enough to shoot at them.

3.

—or Are They Really Meteors?

On February 9, 1913 several thousand people in Canada were treated to a most unusual celestial phenomenon coming toward them from the northwest—a row of four glowing lights, closely followed by a row of three abreast, and by at least a dozen others arranged in similar formation.

The awesome aerial parade continued parallel to the earth for over 2,400 miles. The Canadians were given ample time for detailed observation as it took the glowing streams of lights approximately 3.3 minutes to pass a given point.

Professor C. A. Chant of the University of Toronto, editor of the *Journal of the Royal Astronomical Society of Canada,* later served to collect the multitude of reports that flowed into the Society's offices from both trained scientists and lay observers. Most witnesses of the unique flight stated that the formation had consisted of from fifteen to twenty glowing objects. Astronomers with powerful telescopes reported that each of the "abnormal meteors" were actually clusters of from twenty to forty smaller objects. All observers seemed to agree that the objects were spherical in shape, reddish-gold in color, and were followed by a long tail which measured over 39 miles in length. Everyone testified to the thunder-like roll of sound that accompanied the objects, and slight earth tremors were recorded as the celestial parade passed overhead.

Scientists hypothesized that the objects had been traveling through space, had been caught by the gravitational pull of the earth, and had become temporary satellites until the atmosphere had eventually disintegrated them. The meteor-satellites had passed over some of Canada's largest centers of population, continued across the United States, over the Bermudas, and on into Brazil before they had vanished from sight.

In 1913, it would have been most startling to suggest that the objects might not have been meteors at all but intelligently manned space craft which, far from disintegrating over the northeast tip of Brazil, had made the decision to return to outer space after a partial orbit of the earth. Although it is impossible to make a very strong case either pro-saucer or pro-meteor-satellite at this late date, a most extraordinary incident that took place on the afternoon of the following day adds another dimension to the mystery. Three groups of "solid, dark objects" passed above the city of Toronto. It was then broad daylight and surely, in 1913, it would have been impossible to mistake a sputtering formation of primitive airplanes for anything other than the fragile craft that they were. According to the *Toronto Star:* "They passed from west to east in three groups, and then returned in more scattered formation, seven or eight in all."

Professor Chant, in the *Journal of the Royal Astronomical Society,* had second thoughts about the aerial show in an arithmetical progression and that the tails of the "meteors" had seemed strangely like rocket propulsion.

It would be foolish to assert that every "falling star" is in reality a flying saucer, but a disturbing number of today's scientists blandly write off the sightings of responsible citizens and trained observers as being just another case of the mistaken identity of a meteor or a planet.

One such acid-tongue skeptic was Dr. H. Percy Wilkins, a Fellow of the Royal Astronomical Society and one of the world's most eminent authorities on the moon. Dr. Wilkins had once told an interviewer: "I am not only a skeptic but a firm unbeliever in any such objects."

That was before Dr. Wilkins saw three saucers of his own on an airplane flight to Atlanta, Georgia on June 11, 1954.

In bright sunlight, at an altitude of about 8,000 feet, Dr. Wilkins saw two shiny, oval-shaped objects hovering above two cumulus cloud formations. "They were sharp-edged, glittering like burnished gold in the sunlight," the scientist noted. "Then I noticed a third and similar object, less bright, possibly because it was in the shade of the same cloud mass. Certainly they were not caused by any optical or meteorological peculiarities."

Last year, Dr. Carl Sagan, a top-ranked United States astronomer, saw no reason to be vague about the possibility of extra-terrestrial space craft having visited our planet. "The statistics that we now possess," Dr. Sagan said, "suggest that the Earth has been visited by representatives from various galactic civilizations many times."

Leading exobiologists (scientists who study lifeforms outside the earth) have concluded that in this galaxy alone, there are quite possibly some 640,000,000 life-bearing planets. That figure alone seems staggering, but bear in mind that there are billions of other galaxies.

Dr. Sagan thinks it not the least bit out of line to assume that as many as 1,000,000 planets in this galaxy may support advanced civilizations similar to that of the earth.

"These creatures have doubtlessly been sending explorative expeditions through interstellar space for countless milleniums," Dr. Sagan believes. "It is not out of the question that some kind of base is maintained within the solar system to provide continuity for successive expeditions. An obvious spot for such a base is our own moon."

In November of 1955, Frank Halstead, curator of the University of Minnesota observatory at Duluth, sighted two flying saucers. Accepting the shock to his own theories with the attitude of a true scientist, Halstead remarked: "All over the world credible witnesses are reporting experiences similar to mine. Holding these people up to ridicule does not alter the existing facts. The time is long overdue for accepting the presence of these things, whatever they are, and for dealing with them and the public on a basis of honesty and realism."

And credible witnesses have truly been reporting unidentified flying objects similar to Frank Halstead's for many years. On August 12, 1883, Senor Jose Bonilla, director of the observatory at Zacatecas, Mexico, had set up his camera to photograph sun spots. He got quite a different series of pictures from those he had expected. He has the honor of being the first professional astronomer to take a picture of a flying saucer.

"To my surprise," Senor Bonilla wrote in a scientific journal, "I observed a small luminous body traverse the disc of the sun. I had not recovered from my surprise when the same phenomenon was repeated! And that with such frequency that, in the space of two hours, I counted up to two hundred eighty-three bodies crossing the solar disc.

"Since my camera had already been set up to photograph sun spots, I photographed most of these strange bodies in projection and in profile. Some appear round or spherical, but one notices in the photographs that the bodies are not spherical, but irregular in form."

The world's foremost authority on space travel, Dr. Hermann Oberth, conducted a three-year study of unidentified flying objects for the West German government before the United States put him under contract to head the Jupiter space program. At the termination of his study in June, 1955, the space scientist said: "They (flying saucers) do not originate on this earth and probably do not originate in our solar system, but very likely come from another galaxy. It is our conclusion that they propel themselves by distorting the gravitational field."

At a press conference that Dr. Oberth held in late 1959, after he had completed his contract at Huntsville, Alabama, the German spacemaster tipped the world off that the Air Force is taking the saucers much more seriously than their official position would seem to indicate. Dr. Oberth stated that the United States was trying to duplicate the propulsion system which is presumably used by the unidentified space vehicles.

According to Dr. Oberth: "Considerable success has been attained in this program, and I believe that within five years, men will be able to travel to the moon in craft propelled by electro-magnetic means."

Even if the German scientist was a bit premature in his estimate of the time involved to perfect electro-magnetic travel, the Air Force remains noncommittal on the subject of how far behind Dr. Oberth's projected schedule they might be. And, of course, the obvious question remains: Is it possible that the publicly scoffing Air Force has secretly captured, recovered, or restored a number of unidentified flying objects which would enable them to study the means of saucer propulsion?

4.

The Fiery UFO That Crashed Near Pittsburgh

The official cry of "meteor" went up on December 9, 1965 when, just before sundown, a brilliant orange object crossed the skies from Michigan over Lake Erie, over northeastern Ohio, and crashed in a woods thirty miles south of Pittsburgh, Pennsylvania.

Almost within an hour of the sighting Dr. Paul Annear of Baldwin-Wallace College had announced his opinion that the object was a meteor. The Pentagon was quick to agree with the professor.

The officially pronounced "meteor" had set grass afire over a 1000-foot area when it had crashed. The object had been sighted by several people on the ground and by many experienced commercial and private pilots. Meteors, of course, do not "fly" but are merely falling through space and become visible when friction with the earth's atmosphere causes them to "glow." Meteors are usually first sighted at heights between 30 and 60 miles and "burn out" their glow at about 10 miles. Peculiarly, this particular "meteor" was charted as making a 25-degree turn over Cleveland and was clocked as moving at about 1062.5 miles per hour.

Ivan T. Sanderson, writing for the North American Newspaper Alliance, expressed his dissatisfaction with the official analysis of the fiery object. "So, this object was a meteor; was it? The minimum speed ever recorded for a meteor was 27,000 miles per hour and the maximum was 144,000 per hour, which is to say seven and one-half miles per second and 40 miles per second respectively! Since when have meteors or bolides, which is the name now given to meteors that break up in our atmosphere, started ambling along at 1,062.5 miles per hour?"

Sanderson also thought it most peculiar that the military was taking such a great interest in the "meteor." Bolides crash to earth nearly every day of the year and are ignored as commonplace by all except those amateur enthusiasts who collect chunks of "falling stars." With this particular "meteor," however, "great contingents of specialists from the armed forces arrived at the scene of the fall almost as fast as the State Police got there."

An armed forces' spokesman was quoted as saying: "We don't know what we have here, but there is an unidentified flying object in the woods."

An armed forces' specialist would certainly not commit the layman's blunder of saying that a meteor was a "flying object." And a meteor is certainly not an "unidentified flying object." Meteors have been around for centuries.

So, it appears, have UFO's.

5.

Flying Saucers in Ancient Times

At a meeting of the American Astronautical Society which took place in Washington, D.C. early in 1966, Dr. Carl Sagan of Harvard University suggested the possibility that superspacemen from far beyond "our tiny corner of the universe may have visited earth thousands of times in the past few billions of years. At least one of these visits may have occurred in historical times."

Although such talk smacks of either pulp science-fiction writing or the irrational ravings which certain Air Force officials think symptomatic of all "saucer-nuts," Dr. Sagan enjoys a position of stature in the field of astronomy. It is interesting to note that the Harvard Professor was a confirmed skeptic of the existence of UFO's back in the 1950's. Writing in the *Encyclopedia Americana,* Sagan said that there was no "convincing evidence" that the saucers were of extra-terrestrial origin. The past decade, however, has done much to alter the views of many scientists, and most of the scoffers and skeptics of the Fifties now believe that there must be literally billions of planets in the universe enough like earth to sustain life. Whether technical civilizations superior to ours flourish on these planets or whether the stage of social development is anywhere from that of the cave dwellers to the Greece of Pericles, it seems obvious to most astronomers that we earthlings are not alone.

Other scientists are suggesting that not only are we not alone, but that we may have been "planted" here a billion or so years ago by an extra-terrestrial expedition. Periodically, the celestial gardeners come back to see how their "seed beds" have been progressing.

Dr. Thomas Gold, Professor of Astronomy at Cornell University, was quoted recently as saying: "Life may have been initiated and spread by space travelers who visited earth a billion years ago. From their abandoned microbiological garbage, forms of life proliferated into intelligent beings."

It has also been hypothesized that the famed "missing-link" which lies between the highest anthropoid and the lowest human being will never be found because it has never existed. Mankind's first parents, according to this theory, might have been a marooned party of space travelers. This may sound like the old science-fiction chestnut, but sober scientists have begun to talk very seriously about that oft-used plot as being a very real possibility worthy of intelligent discussion.

As an alternate theory, some scientists have enlivened another familiar fictional gimmick, that of the earlier, advanced civilization that fled this planet for another to escape some impending disaster, such as the sinking of their continent or the advent of an ice age. The legends of Atlantis and other lost continents have lingered in man's collective store of myths for centuries. Perhaps, some scientists are suggesting, there is more than a little truth in the legends that an ultra-sophisticated civilization flourished on this planet thousands of years ago.

Dr. Sagan told his fellow astronomers at the meeting of the American Astronautical Society that the best place to look for evidence of other technical civilizations on other planets in this or other galaxies would be right here on earth.

As a physical substantiation to the theories espoused by Dr. Sagan and other exiobiologists and astronomers, consider the gold thread that was found embedded in eight feet of rock near Rutherford Mills, England on June 22, 1844 or the iron nail that was discovered in a block of stone in the Kingoodie Quarry in North Britain the same year. Geological formations, in which the hand- or machine-crafted artifacts were found, date from the Paleocene epoch—50,000,000 years before man, as we know him, existed.

A length of gold thread and an iron nail—are they clues to visitors from outer space who arrived and settled or explored the earth millions of years before civilized man appeared on this planet? Archeologists insist that there are no traces of man with any rudiments of sophistication before 7000 B.C. Man had not perfected the fashioning of elementary tools until 4000 B.C. How then does anyone explain the thread and the nail (and there have been other such "artifacts") found in rock strata at least 60,000,000 years old?

If it is true, as Charles Fort once remarked, that "we are property," then it would not be difficult to accept the hypothesis that the waves of UFO's are simply expeditions come to check up on their "investment." Those who have studied classical texts with an eye for possible UFO-influenced passages have concluded that ancient peoples were indeed aware of periodic visitations and interpreted them in the language of their own limited technology.

One of the most popular "sightings" which exobiologists are re-evaluating is that of the prophet Ezekial and his fiery wheel "way up in de middle of de air," as the popular Negro spiritual celebrates the visitation. If the incident is read as a Hebrew prophet expressing an encounter with an unidentified flying object in poetic rather than literal language, the scientists, who are re-examining Ezekial's original words, may find much to reward their efforts.

As translated in the Revised Standard Version of the *Bible* (Ezekial 1:4-28): "As I looked, behold, a stormy wind came out of the north, and a great cloud, with brightness round about it, and fire flashing forth continually, and in the midst of the fire, as it were gleaming bronze. And from the midst of it came the likeness of four living creatures . . . they had the form of men, but each had four faces, and each of them had four wings. Their legs were straight and the soles of their feet were like the sole of a calf's foot; and they sparkled like burnished bronze . . . In the midst of the living creatures there was something that looked like burning coals of fire, like torches moving to and fro among the living creatures;

and the fire was bright, and out of the fire went forth lightning . . . Now as I looked at the living creatures, I saw a wheel upon the earth beside the living creatures, one for each of the four of them. As for the appearance of the wheels and their construction: . . . like a gleaming of a chrysolite; and the four had the same likeness, their construction being as it were a wheel within a wheel . . . The four wheels had rims and they had spokes; and their rims were full of eyes round about. (Indeed, a good description of a flying saucer. Especially if one acknowledges the rows of eyes to be windows.) Over the heads of the living creatures there was the likeness of a firmament, shining like crystal . . ."

One thinks instantly of a non-oxygen breathing alien in his clear helmet. The globular helmet may also have led the prophet to conclude that the creatures had "four faces."

The Mayans have a legend about a giant eagle that came out of the sky "with the roar of a lion." Again we are led to consider that the myth might have an alien-reality when we read: "From her beak come four creatures, strange to our tribe, who did not breathe the air we breathe."

W. Raymond Drake has analyzed the works of fifty great classical writers, including Julius Obsequens, Livy, Pliny, Dio Cassius and Cicero. He has found dozens of references to celestial phenomena, which comprise a 2000-year record of ancient UFO sightings. Among the phenomena that Drake noted were lights and shields in the sky, fiery globes, ships, men, armies, two or more moons, two or more suns, new stars, falling lights, unknown voices, "gods" descending to earth, and "men" ascending to the sky.

In the December, 1964 issue of *Fate* magazine, Drake writes: "Our theologians dismiss the ancient Gods as anthropomorphisms of natural forces, as if entire races for hundreds of years would base their daily lives on lightning and thunderbolts! Yet logic suggests that the old Gods of Egypt, Greece, Rome, Scandinavia, and Mexico were not disembodied spirits or anthropomorphic symbolisms but actual spacemen from the skies. It seems that after the great catastrophes remembered in the legends, the 'Gods' withdrew and henceforth have been content merely to survey the Earth, except for an occasional intervention in human affairs."

Professor M. M. Agrest, in an article in the *Literaturya Gazette,* expressed his belief that the remains of Sodom and Gomorrah bear evidence that the ancient twin cities of wickedness were destroyed in a pre-paleolithic nuclear explosion. Professor Agrest, a Russian physicist, also maintains that a strange rock platform in Lebanon, whose origin and original purpose have baffled archeologists and geologists for several years, was constructed by aliens as a launching pad.

Agrest shares Dr. Sagan's view that the best place to look for evidence of alien peoples is right here on earth. As additional "evidence," the Russian scientist offers the existence of teklites, strange glasslike stones which contain radioactive isotopes of aluminum and beryllium and might be the refuse of alien experiments conducted on our planet a few million years ago; "round head" monuments and artworks, which could be representations of space visitors; ancient religions and "gods" that descend to earth and "men" who are taken alive into the skies; scientific treatises from antiquity, which are so advanced in comparison to the primitive knowledge of surrounding cultures that special tutoring from advanced aliens is suggested.

Far from scoffing at their fellow scientist's theory of alien visitations before and during the evolution of man, a crew of Russian exobiologists is currently wandering the world seeking additional artifacts that might offer a clue to extra-terrestrial guidance (or interference) of this planet's properties and potentialities. The team of Soviet scientists is also attempting to locate other traces of pre-1945 nuclear explosions.

An increasing number of scientists are reading the myths and legends of ancient peoples with renewed interest, as they search for any sign that might lead to an important discovery, such as the unearthing of a cache of alien artifacts several millions years old. And passages such as this one, translated from the Sanskrit of 2,000 years ago, are being valued for more than their poetic symbolism: "When dawn broke, Rama climbed aboard the aircraft, which was called *Pushpaka* and stood ready to depart. The craft was large, brightly painted, and self-propelled. It had two decks, many windows, and cabins. As it lifted majestically into the air and leveled off, it gave forth a melodious hum."

6.

Flying Saucers and Disappearing People

Twelve-year-old Raimunda da Silva of Diamantina, Brazil has never heard of flying saucers, bug-eyed monsters, or Buck Rogers. He has never read a Flash Gordon comic book—because he is illiterate—or watched *Lost in Space* on a TV set—because he is unaware of electricity, not to mention radio or television. Yet it was this same unsophisticated boy who ran into police headquarters on August 20, 1962 and told the incredulous officers that his father had been taken away by two giant balls that sparked fire and puffed out yellow smoke.

It had been shortly after dawn when Raimunda had first seen the weird shadow of the being that had observed him, his father, Rivalino de Silva, and his two brothers, Fatimo, six, and Dirceu, two. The creature "was not shaped like a human being," Raimunda told the authorities, and it seemed to float rather than walk. As the creature had glided out of the bedroom Raimunda shared with his father, the boy swore that he had heard it say: "Rivalino is in here. He must be destroyed."

Rivalino de Silva had begun to move as if he were entranced. He opened the front door and Raimunda saw him begin to walk toward two large globes that floated about six or seven feet above the ground. The objects had made a humming sound and flickered a strange kind of fire. The boy called to his father, but Rivalino continued to draw closer to the hovering discs. Then, before Raimunda's horrified eyes, the globes emitted a heavy yellow smoke, that completely enveloped his father's body. When the smoke cleared, the balls had disappeared and so had Rivalino da Silva.

Police began an immediate investigation. At the da Silva hut, the officers found a strange, cleanly swept area in the dust that was about 16 feet in diameter. There were no footprints or tracks of any kind in the area. The investigating officers did find a few drops of blood a little over 160 feet from the da Silva home. Laboratory analysis later classified the blood as that of a human, but whether or not the fluid had come from Rivalino da Silva was impossible to determine since there was no record of da Silva's blood type.

Police are pretty much the same the world over. To the officer in the field, a single fact is better than a dozen theories. The authorities began to conduct the investigation as if they were dealing with a murder case.

Somewhat cruelly, the police began to suspect the now orphaned boys—their mother had died about a year before—of having killed their father and disposed of his body. The suggestion of three boys, ranging in age from twelve to two, having committed a murder, although seemingly ludicrous, is not without precedent. The officers tried a number of psychological ploys, carefully crafted to trick Raimunda into a confession, but the spindly 12-year-old stuck resolutely to his story of the smoking globes and the floating shadow. At last the officers themselves became touched by the obvious sincerity of the boy's grief and began to conduct an investigation along lines they considered utterly fantastic. Strangely enough, they began to turn up corroborating testimony of an extremely eerie nature.

A fisherman testified that he had seen two peculiar, ball-shaped aircraft circling over the da Silva home on the evening of August 19th. Two miner friends of Rivalino da Silva's had laughed at him on August 17th when he had told them about coming upon "two strange persons, about three feet tall, digging a hole in the earth." Now, after their friend had disappeared, the miners had had second thoughts about da Silva's "queer story" and wondered if there might not be some connection between his mysterious disappearance and his sighting of the "two strange persons."

Lt. Wilson Lisboa's report of the investigation was published in two Brazilian newspapers, Belo Horizonte's *Diario de Minas* and the Rio de Janeiro *Correio da Manha*. In the report, a Dr. Giovani Pereia in Diamantina was quoted as saying that he had seen an object similar to the one that had allegedly swooped off with Rivalino da Silva above his own house two months earlier. The doctor hadn't mentioned the object before, because, wisely, he knew that no one would believe him.

Four days after da Silva's celestial abduction, more than fifty people, including the Chief of Police, witnessed the flight of a "large round ball-shaped object" over the nearby town of Gouveia.

The villagers of Brasila de Minas were thrown into a state of near-panic when, on August 28th, an object that looked "like a big, glowing soccer ball" hovered over the town's church steeple for several minutes. The residents of the tiny communities were all talking of the mysterious "kidnapping" of Rivalino da Silva, and the continued appearances of the UFO's seemed only to indicate that the creatures were seeking additional victims.

Meanwhile, Lieutenant Lisboa had ordered a psychiatric examination of Raimunda da Silva. The psychiatrist, Dr. Joao Antunes de Oliveiera, told reporters: "I don't wish to discuss the facts in this case. They are beyond my competence. But I can tell you that the boy is normal and is telling what he thinks to be the truth."

A month after Rivalino's bizarre disappearance, the police officially closed the case. They had uncovered no body, no clues, absolutely no evidence or information pertinent to the whereabouts or the fate of the unfortunate man. Police officer Clemente told reporters: "No one expects to find a satisfactory explanation with regard to Mr. da Silva's disappearance."

Could it be that Rivalino da Silva had accidentally stumbled upon alien beings engaged in some activity which they had decreed must be kept secret? He had told his friends that he had seen "two strange persons digging a hole in the earth." Had the creatures been planting something in the fertile Brazilian soil? Or had da Silva stumbled upon an alien burial party? His son, Raimunda, insisted to police that he had heard "voices" outside the hut that morning agreeing that Rivalino was in the house and that he must be destroyed. The mission of the strange "shadow," which Raimunda had seen in the bedroom that he had shared with his father, seemed to be to establish positive identification of Rivalino. Had this poor Brazilian "seen too much," and thereby endangered the security of an alien expedition to earth? Or have outer-space creatures been periodically plucking up earthlings for study and interrogation?

It was on Christmas Eve, 1909, that "they" took 11-year-old Oliver Thomas up into the sky.

Five inches of fresh snow had fallen that day and evening and it was turning cold outside. Around the cheery hearth of farmer Owen Thomas, however, it was warm and comforting and a dozen contented people roasted chestnuts in the hot embers and sang carols as they waited for the clock to chime in Christmas Day. In addition to their family, the Thomases had been joined by their close friends. The minister and his wife were there along with the local veterinarian, and an auctioneer from a nearby village.

At about eleven o'clock, Owen Thomas noticed that the water bucket needed filling. "Oliver, lad," the Welsh farmer said to his son, "we'll be needing some more water. It's yet an hour 'til midnight, and throats will soon be parched from singing."

Ever the obedient son, Oliver slipped into his boots and his heavy overcoat. He had not been gone ten seconds when the entire party heard the boy scream for help.

The minister grabbed a paraffin lantern as everyone rushed outside to see what could possibly have happened to the boy. The lantern's sputtering light pushed back the darkness from the snowy yard, but Oliver was nowhere to be seen. He was, however, amply heard.

"They've got me! Help, help! They've got me!" Oliver's voice was heard to scream again and again.

"His voice seems to be coming from the sky!" the minister said, casting the feeble beam of the paraffin lantern into the black, starless sky above them.

Oliver's parents were on the edge of hysteria as they desperately sought a glimpse of their son. He was simply not to be seen and his cries for help became weaker and weaker. At last, there was nothing left but the echo of the boy's screams in the stillness of the cold winter night.

With the deep, virgin snow as witness, the horror-struck Thomas family and their friends could see by Oliver's footsteps that he had gone about 75 feet across the yard toward the well, when his tracks stopped as suddenly as if he had been yanked upwards by a snare rope. The wooden bucket that he had carried lay about fifteen feet away from the footprints. There were no other tracks or impressions of any kind in the unblemished snow.

As Christmas Day was welcomed in by the chiming of church bells in the Brecon valley, the minister offered a prayer of hope for the sobbing and grief-stricken Thomas family. Their wonderful Welsh Christmas Eve party had been turned into a nightmare of terror by some unknown assailants.

The next day, police officials from the nearby town of Rhayader formed a searching party and completely scoured the countryside. They probed the well with grappling hooks and thoroughly interrogated all those who had been present on the preceding evening. In spite of the fact that it was obvious from Oliver's footsteps in the snow that he had never reached the well or turned aside from the straight line that he was keeping toward his destination, the police insisted upon satisfying themselves with a complete investigation.

There was only one conclusion that the authorities were able to render: Oliver Thomas had inexplicably vanished —straight up.

But where had Oliver gone and what or who had taken him? The boy was much too heavy for any known bird to have snatched, certainly too large for any of the birds of Wales. At the 1909 stage in their development, airplanes had enough difficulty getting themselves airborne without plucking up unwilling passengers by means of some kind of skyhook.

Eleven people heard Oliver Thomas shout: "They've got me!"

Choice of words when one panics is very important and always revealing. It would seem that the boy had got a good look at the "they" who were snatching him up, or else it seems likely that he would have shouted that an "it," a "something," or "a giant bird" had got him. But even in his great fright, young Oliver Thomas repeated over and over again that "they" had him.

"They" also, occasionally, snatch animals.

On the afternoon of April 21, 1897 a prosperous cattleman near Yates Center, Kansas reported to authorities that an airship had hauled one of his heifers up into its hold. The rancher, Alexander Hamilton, was a former member of the state legislature and was known across Kansas as a man of total veracity.

Hamilton told the *Farmer's Advocate* for its April 23rd issue: "Last Monday night, about 10:30, we were awakened by a noise among the cattle . . . upon going to the door, I saw to my utter astonishment an airship slowly descending upon my cow lot, about 40 rods from the house.

"Calling my tenant, Gid Heslip, and my son, Wall, we seized some axes and ran to the corral. Meanwhile, the ship had been gently descending until it was not more than 30 feet above the ground, and we came up to within 50 yards of it. It consisted of a great cigar-shaped portion possibly 300 feet long with a carriage underneath.

"The carriage was made of panels of glass or other transparent substance, alternating with a narrow strip of some other material. It was brilliantly lighted within . . . It was occupied by six of the strangest beings I ever saw. There were two men, a woman and three children. They were jabbering together but we could not understand a syllable they said.

". . . upon catching sight of us, they turned on some unknown power, and a great turbine wheel about 30 feet in diameter, which was slowly revolving around the craft, began to buzz . . . and rose as lightly as a bird.

"When about 30 feet above us, it seemed to pause, and

hover directly over a three-year-old heifer . . . Going to her we found a cable about half an inch in thickness, made of red material, fastened in a slip knot around her neck, one end passing up to the vessel. . . .

"We tried to get it off but could not . . . we stood in amazement to see ship, cow, and all rise slowly and sail off, disappearing in the northwest. We went home but I was so frightened I could not sleep but arose early Tuesday morning, mounted my horse and started out to find some trace of my cow, but coming back to LeRoy in the evening found that Lank Thomas, who lives in Coffey County about three or four miles west of LeRoy, had found the hide, legs and head in his field that day."

Eleven prominent citizens of the area signed an affidavit testifying to Alexander Hamilton's reputation for truthfulness and prefaced their signatures with these remarks: "As there are now, always have been, and always will be skeptics and unbelievers, whenever the truth of anything bordering on the improbable is presented, and knowing that some ignorant or suspicious people will doubt the truthfulness of the above (Hamilton's) statement, now, therefore, we, the undersigned, do hereby make the following affidavit. That we have known Alexander Hamilton from 15 to 30 years and that for truth and veracity we have never heard his word questioned and that we do verily believe his statement to be true and correct."

Much more ambitious than the kidnapping of an 11-year-old boy or the celestial rustling of a little fresh beef was the snatching of an entire British regiment in August of 1915.

The incident was witnessed by 22 men of No. 3 Section of the 1st Division Field Company N.Z.E.F. from their position in the trenches on Rhododendron Spur near Suvla Bay, Anzac. The survivors of this particular campaign recently signed an affidavit testifying to the mass kidnapping at their Fiftieth Jubilee of the Anzac Landing. In World War I, a British regiment consisted of anywhere from 800 to 4,000 men. Surely, this large-scale saucer-snatch must set the record for an UFO kidnapping.

According to Mr. F. Reichart of New Zealand, one of the eye-witnesses to the mysterious disappearance, the troops in the trenches had noticed six to eight large "loaf of bread-shaped clouds of a light-grey color" at dawn that morning. The soldiers had commented on the fact that the light breeze that was blowing that morning did nothing to alter the position of these particular clouds, which appeared to be solid in structure.

As the strange clouds hovered above a dry creek bed, the One-Fourth Norfolk Regiment were seen to be marching up the creek bed, ostensibly to reinforce the men in the trenches on Hill 60. One of the large clouds lowered itself into the path of the marching troops, and the soldiers on the hill watched in amazement as their reinforcements walked into the cloud but never emerged from it!

After the last of the Norfolk Regiment had marched "into the cloud," the large, grey "loaf of bread" rose into the air, rejoined the clouds that had remained hovering above it, and, while the soldiers in the trenches watched in horror, the eight clouds moved off against the wind.

Officially, the One-Fourth Norfolk Regiment was listed as having been destroyed by the Turkish Army, its men either captured, killed, or missing in action.

Ex-trooper F. Reichart, quoted in the March, 1966 issue of *Flying Saucers* magazine, says: "On Turkey's surrender in 1918, the first thing the British authorities demanded of the Turks was the return of the Regiment, supposing them captured. Turkey replied that she had neither captured this regiment nor made contact with it and did not know that the Regiment existed."

Reichart goes on to state that such incidents are not unique in the files of the British Army. According to Reichart, the official histories record a similar disappearance of a British platoon in the Sudan in 1898. Search parties in the Khyber Pass area, also in 1898, reported the mysterious disappearance of a company of British Engineers. Tracks of the vanished men ended abruptly, "the footmarks all pointed straight ahead, but nothing beyond, sideways, or backwards."

7.

The Busy Saucer Summer of 1965

Until 1965, 1952 had been the biggest year for flying saucers with a record 1,501 sightings. Official sightings for 1965's busy saucer summer are still being weighed and evaluated, but it appears that several thousand UFO's of all sizes, shapes, and weird descriptions were spotted by what the Air Force had grudgingly to admit were "above average" saucer viewers. Never before had so many people become so worked up about UFO's, and never before had the nation's newspapers become so openly critical of the Air Force's method of handily explaining away every sighting with the same tired dismissals of weather balloons and the planet Venus. Last summer, everyone was talking about flying saucers—most, for the first time, seriously. People were beginning to demand that something be done about the strange interlopers from the skies. Citizens insisted that Air Force and government officials tell all that they might know about unidentified flying objects. In the summer of 1965 UFO's became subject to everyone's scrutiny and were at last removed, in the average man's mind, from the exclusive province of the crank, kook, or cultist. For the first time, one could discuss flying saucers at a cocktail party without being immediately censured and labeled "some kind of a nut."

The massive saucer flap ("flap" being Air Force jargon for large groups of people acting in a confused manner, just a few degrees below panic) began on July 1st, when, almost simultaneously, an unidentified flying object was reported as having been sighted over France, and a saucer over the Santa Maria airport in the Azores stopped all electric clocks.

On July 3rd, Chilean, British, and Argentine personnel stationed in the Antarctic reported seeing several glowing objects in the sky. Argentina stated that the objects had interfered with instruments measuring magnetic fields.

The Antarctic reports were made even more exciting on July 9th, when Mario Jahn Barrera, commander of the Chilean base, radioed that a corporal had taken color pictures of a UFO. Commander Barrera described the object as "a mysterious, lens-shaped flying object, maneuvering and moving at great speed . . . (in color) yellowish red, changing to green, yellow, and orange."

Commander Barrera told the Chilean Defense Ministry by radio. "It was something real, an object that moved at amazing speed, maneuvered quickly and gave off a blue-green sheen. It also caused interference in the electro-magnetic apparatus of an Argentine base which is facing ours on a nearby small island."

"It would zigzag quickly. Then it stopped, and we promptly reached for field glasses, telescopes, anything at hand to sight it. We watched as it remained quietly there for about 20 minutes.

"I can say that it was not a star, because its movement was rapid and continuous. As to being an aircraft, I don't think so. I am an air force man and from what I know about aircraft, there is nothing like it, because of its shape, the speed, and maneuverability."

A navy communique from the commander of the Argentine base substantiated Barrera's report. "The characteristics of the object and its movement show that it was neither balloon, nor star, nor aircraft," said Lt. Daniel Perisse.

"The object was seen under weather conditions that could be considered exceptional at this time of the year: A clear sky, some isolated strato-cumulus, the moon visible in the waning quarter.

"The meteorologist of the detachment and 10 other men watched the object for a period of some 15 to 20 minutes. Photographs were taken . . . I doubt if the pictures will be any good because they were taken in total darkness."

Residents of a penthouse apartment in the Copacabana section of Rio de Janeiro were given a firsthand look at one of the objects about which they had been reading in the papers when a "soundless, round object with eight portholes" slowly crossed the sky about 7:00 P.M. on July 10th.

At Lisbon, Portugal on July 11th, UFO's were sighted by several people, who described the objects as looking like "flattened balloons." Manuel Fernandes and his wife agreed that their object resembled "a plate turned over. The saucer stopped at a rather high altitude, for about three minutes, then, with an incredible velocity, sped toward the north."

A spokesman for the Villa do Porto weather bureau claimed that the energy field of a "cylindrical white object," moving at an altitude of 24,000 to 30,000 feet, "stopped the bureau's electro-magnetic clocks."

On July 15th, the saucers had once again dipped "down-under," this time to Canberra, Australia. The United States, via its Mariner space probe, was supposed to be getting all the attention, as pictures from Mars were being relayed back to earth. At the Canberra airport, however, a mysterious glowing object was doing its best to divert the attention of the air traffic control officers.

Six members of a traffic control crew said that the glowing UFO hung suspended at about 5,000 feet for at least 40 minutes. When the sun glinted off it, it became clearly visible. It disappeared when an Air Force plane was sent out to identify it.

Certain experts began to speculate on the possibility that the unusual difficulties experienced by the Tidninbilla tracking station before it was able to pick up the signals from the Mariner had anything to do with the appearance of the UFO.

On July 17th, a flying saucer was seen hovering over the Rio Plata River that divides Argentina and Uruguay. Six persons walking on a deserted beach near Colonia, Uruguay reported seeing the UFO. Simultaneous with this report was the sighting of a formation of objects over Buenos Aires.

Father Benito Reyna, S.J., a Jesuit priest-astronomer and professor of mathematics at Salvador University in Buenos Aires, said that he had seen several UFO's in Argentine skies. Father Reyna, an astronomer with over 30 years' experience, was not likely to confuse a UFO with anything that is supposed to be in the heavens.

"The first time I saw UFO's I was in Cordoba," Father Reyna told reporters. "With the help of my telescope, I was able to follow their flight clearly and to note their shape and color, predominantly white, yellow, red, and blue hues.

"Then last March I saw them on two successive nights in San Miguel. At that time Echo II was orbiting the earth and I believe the crew of the flying saucer was closely following the U.S. man-made satellite to study its characteristics.

"We are not certain of the existence of other intelligent beings similar to ourselves, but on the other hand, we have no evidence to the contrary," said Father Reyna.

Strangely enough, Astronaut James McDivitt claimed to have photographed an unknown flying object while on the Gemini-4 spaceflight. On his second full day in orbit, McDivitt transmitted that he had seen something "with big arms sticking out." The astronaut took several feet of film of the mystery object with his movie camera and one snap with his Hasselblad still camera. The developed film gave evidence of nothing that looked remotely like either an already-placed U.S. or Russian satellite or the flying object that McDivitt had described.

Space Agency officials issued a statement that McDivitt had seen the 23,100-pound Pegasus-2, which might be considered to have "big arms sticking out." It must be noted, however, that Pegasus-2 was 1,200 miles away at the time when McDivitt declared that his object was "about 20 miles away and closing fast."

A brilliant object streaked across the Pittsburgh, Pennsylvania skies at extremely high speed on the night of July 24th. Police switchboards became jammed with calls of sightings by nervous citizens. Nearly all residents of the Pittsburgh area described the object as a white-hot light with an orange tail.

Personnel at radar stations in North Dakota, Minnesota, and Luther Air Station in Canada reported spotting several UFO's at varying altitudes of 5,200 to 17,000 feet. Luther Air Station said that its radar had become electrically jammed by the mysterious objects.

Jet interceptors gave chase to the UFO's over Duluth, Minnesota but were unable to match the speeds of the glowing objects.

It seemed as though the one-night excursion to North America may only have been in the nature of a scouting expedition. On July 25th, the UFO's were once again reported in South America—this time at Lima, Peru.

A night watchman at the Electric Center in Lima said that at 3:00 A.M. he was alerted by a "bubbling and buzzing sound" which came from a large round object which hovered above the plant's parking lot. He estimated the size of the UFO to be about 15 feet in diameter. It had windows which gave off intermittent colored lights, and the globe-shaped object had a kind of turret on its top which rotated a protruding metal arm, as if it were some kind of scanning device. The UFO had taken off immediately when the watchman had appeared at the window of the Electric Center.

The residents of Chinchero, Peru reported a disc-shaped object hovering above their city for an entire hour on July 28th.

On the same day in Maracaibo, Venezuela, three UFO's were tracked on radar at the Grano de Oro airport. The flying saucers were impossible to ignore as they hovered above the main runway while an instructor in radar operation conducted class for new personnel of the Control Tower.

"I can't say whether they were saucers or not," the instructor told newsmen. "I only know that they were strange objects and they showed on the radar screen.

They had an elongated shape like a cigar, but with a bulge in the center."

On July 30th, patrons leaving a movie theater in Cumana, Venezuela were treated to an added attraction as an object that gave off yellowish lights and "looked like a saucer wrapped in flames" dipped out of the sky. Minutes later, the seaside resort of Lecheria, over 60 miles away, reported that the flaming object had passed over its beaches.

An unsubstantiated report from Santiago, Chile had a UFO landing in the city, but a substantially witnessed observation of a flying saucer on the ground came from Puerto Monte, Chile. There, on July 30th, more than 15 persons were maintaining a death watch over the body of a child who had been fatally injured in a street accident. Suddenly the house in which they sat became illuminated by a purplish light. Several of the mourners stepped outside to determine the cause of the strange illumination. They were stunned to see a "strange machine" that hovered just a few inches above the street. Their collective description of the object was a confused one, because shortly after their arrival, the UFO had emitted a blinding light and had blasted off with a noisy roar. Although their individual descriptions of what they had seen might have varied, they were all agreed on one basic point: a "strange machine" had landed very near them.

By July 30th, the saucers seemed ready to invade the United States on a full scale, thereby setting off a rash of sightings that for sheer bulk and individual drama surpassed even the big saucer year of 1952.

Spokane, Washington reported the first UFO's of the summer's bumper crop of celestial phenomena. The citizens of Spokane saw two strange objects in their skies, both bluish white with a slight reddish tinge and oblong in shape.

The sheriff's office declared the objects to be weather

balloons until the U.S. Weather Bureau informed the law officers that there were no balloons in the area.

A spokesman for Fairchild Air Force Base admitted that "a light in the sky had been observed by base personnel," but he went on to deny reports that fighter planes had been dispatched to investigate the light.

On Sunday night, August 1st, authorities in portions of Texas, New Mexico, Oklahoma, and Kansas were deluged with reports of UFO's.

The Sedgewick County Sheriff's office at Wichita announced to newsmen that the weather bureau had tracked "several of them at altitudes of 6,000 to 9,000 feet."

The Oklahoma Highway Patrol stated that Tinker Air Force Base in Oklahoma City was tracking as many as four of the unidentified flying objects on its radar screens at one time. Operators estimated their altitude at about 22,000 feet. Newsmen contacted a spokesman for the Air Force Base, but he refused to confirm or deny the radar observations. Information Officer Lt. John Walmsly told the press: "The reported sightings this evening will be investigated by air force personnel."

The Oklahoma Highway Patrol was much less reluctant to comment on the reality of the UFO's than the Air Force had been. Police officers in three different patrol cars had reported observing saucers flying in diamond-shaped formations for about 30 minutes in the Shawnee area. In an official release, the patrol said that the officers had described the UFO's as changing in color from red to white to blue-green.

A dispatcher for the Sedgwick County, Kansas, sheriff's office was quoted as saying: "I was a disbeliever, but I saw something up there tonight and so did other observers at the Weather Bureau and McConnell Air Force Base."

John Shockley, a Wichita Weather Bureau observer, tracked several UFO's between 2:00 and 6:00 A.M. at altitudes of between 6,000 and 9,000 feet and said that one "looked about the size of a Cessna airplane on the screen."

In a tape-recorded interview for Wichita's radio station KFH, Police Officer Edward Roberts told of sighting one of the objects east of the airport. "We stood on top of the car," Officer Roberts said. "You could see the object with the naked eye. It looked like it was on the ground or hovering just above the ground . . . it was red, greenish-blue and yellowish white . . . about 100 yards long and egg-shaped."

Dan Carter, Deputy Sheriff of Canyon, Texas, told newsmen that at first he had thought that "a plane had exploded in the air. Then the object appeared to go south."

On Monday, August 2nd, the Air Force made an official evaluation of the weekend that had been literally drenched with UFO reports. As their "preliminary conclusion," the Air Force said that people who thought that they had seen flying saucers probably were seeing stars.

"Initial study of reports received from Texas, New Mexico, Oklahoma, and Kansas would indicate that the observations were astrological in nature," the official pronunciamento read.

Specifically, the Air Force declared that the celestial culprits responsible for the UFO flap were the planet Jupiter and some assorted stars.

Robert Risser, director of the Oklahoma Science and Art Foundation Planetarium in Oklahoma City, spoke out and said that observers in Oklahoma had definitely not seen the planet or stars that the Air Force had listed.

"That is as far from the truth as you can get," Risser stated bluntly. "Somebody has made a mistake. These stars and planets are on the *opposite side* of the earth from Oklahoma City at this time of the year."

The Fort Worth, Texas *Star Telegram* proclaimed: "They can stop kidding us now about there being no such things as 'flying saucers.'

"Too many people of obviously sound mind saw and reported them independently from too many separate localities. Their descriptions of what they saw were too similar to one another and too unlike any familiar object.

"And it's going to take more than a statistical report on how many reported 'saucers' have turned out to be jets and weather balloons to convince us otherwise."

The *Denver Post* took immediate issue with the Air Force analysis of the hectic saucer weekend. "Stars of a summer night don't cause blips on ordinary radar, and those things observed on the radar screens of the Wichita weather bureau understandably have caused more than the usual seasonal excitement over unidentified flying objects.

"The blips indicated the same kind of objects that were reported over at least six western states, including Colorado and Wyoming. Maybe it's time for more people to get serious about the UFO question.

"But we'll take our tongue out of our cheek long enough to urge that the Air Force look into this latest flurry of sightings and then tell us something besides the fact that they are under investigation."

On August 4th, a 23-year-old high school English teacher in Sioux City, Iowa told authorities: "Anyone who would say this is a star would be out of his mind."

At least half a dozen persons called Sioux City police, the U.S. weather station, and news media to report that they had seen "things in the sky" between 9:30 and 10:45 P.M. Most of the callers said that the objects were bright red and moved with a great burst of speed.

The teacher, who wished to remain unidentified, told authorities that he and his wife had spotted a bright, yellowish light that zig-zagged slightly and moved at an extremely high rate of speed. He was certain that it wasn't an airplane because he had turned off his engine and got out of the car to "try to listen to some kind of engine sounds. There weren't any."

The object was "wedge-shaped," according to the teacher, and had been witnessed by several other persons in the area.

Mrs. Ray LeFebvere of Sioux City said that she had seen a red light along with two or three smaller lights moving very fast in the sky. "It wasn't a star and it wasn't an airplane," Mrs. LeFebvere insisted.

Newspapers as well as private citizens continued to be offended by the Air Force's official disclaimers of the increasingly frequent sightings. The Richmond, Virginia *News-Leader* editorialized: "Project Bluebook officials, the Air Force people who are supposed to identify mysterious objects in the sky, are seeing stars again. An Air Force spokesman said that glowing aerial objects reported over a four-state Western area were astronomical in nature. The planet Jupiter and the stars Betelguese, Rigel, Aldebaran and Capella, were said by the Pentagon spokesman to be the likely objects sighted.

"This finding sent surprised professional astronomers back to their charts, only to confirm their original beliefs: At the time the Air Force reported the stars visible from the United States, they were in fact visible only from the other side of the world . . ."

The *News-Leader* concluded in a tone of righteous indignation that such clumsy and feeble attempts by the Air Force to "dismiss the reported sightings under the rationale as exhibited by Project Blue book won't solve the mystery," but, they maintained, would "serve only to heighten the suspicion that there's something out there the Air Force doesn't want us to know about."

Don Tennopir, a 44-year-old truck driver from Beatrice, Oklahoma, found out the hard way that "there's something out there" and whether the Air Force wants us to know about it or not, he, personally, never wants to learn another thing about flying saucers.

Pale and shaken, the truckdriver told his story to police officials and newsmen: "I was driving north of Highway 15 about 25 miles south of Abilene. I was carrying a full load of peanuts and was enroute to Lincoln, Nebraska. I guess it was about 1:30 A.M. when all of a sudden the lights on my truck went out. Then came back on, then off, then back on again.

"About this time, this thing, saucer, or whatever, went over my truck with a sizzling or wind-like blowing sound.

It scared the hell out of me. It seemed to almost touch the cab, maybe it was 20 feet in the air, and it just swooped down over the road and hovered there not more than 100 feet in front of me.

"I tell you I was standing on those brakes. I just didn't know what was happening. It looked like it was going to fall right in the middle of the road, but it didn't.

"I got my rig stopped and about that time this thing raised up a bit and slowly took off to the west and then headed south. I don't know how long it was there. It seemed longer than 20 seconds, but I was just too damned scared to tell time.

"The thing looked round to me. I'd guess it was about 14 or 15 feet in diameter and sore of orange-colored. It shot off reddish rays, kind of in spurts. The rays weren't really steady, kind of flashing.

"The object appeared to be like a saucer. I'd guess it was about two feet thick and the edge was round. There was a hump, or something like that in the middle. This hump stuck up about four feet or so. There was a dark spot in the hump, and this might have been a window or something. I just don't know."

A Lincoln, Nebraska train crew working near Weeping Water also had the somewhat dubious privilege of observing a UFO at close range, as it hovered above them for about three minutes.

"And we were all stone-cold sober," Don Huff, 19, a brakeman for the Missouri-Pacific Railroad, told newsmen. "It came out of the north, passed about two miles in front of the train, went south a little way toward the hills, and then returned and hovered at an altitude of about one mile."

Other crew members of the work train who saw the saucer were Aca Butler, the conductor; George Barton, the engineer, and R. D. Rue, a brakeman.

Rue saw the UFO first and called it to the attention of Barton and Huff. Butler was riding at the rear of the train, but he told newsmen that he had also seen the object.

"After hovering over us for a time, the thing dipped down, as if taking a look at us," Huff said. "I could see the top of the craft when it dipped. I looked for outlines of a doorway or some kind of hatch but couldn't see any."

The men agreed that the outer rim of the object had been equipped with several lights that blinked steadily in a clock-wise pattern. It left no smoke trail and had no visible means of propulsion.

"At first we thought it was a dirigible," Huff said. "But when it tipped and came down, we sure changed our minds."

On August 3rd, Minneapolis, Minnesota had its official hands full juggling reports of UFO's that "bobbed, dipped, hovered, stopped, jerked along and sped away."

Again, Air Force officials calmly informed the residents of the Minneapolis area that they had seen "unusually bright stars which seemed to change colors because of the unusually clear skies. Also, there had been a number of B-52 military aircraft in the area."

The *Minneapolis Star* retaliated that "unusually bright stars and B-52's are not strange multi-colored objects that bounce up and down like yo-yo's, hover, dart away at breakneck speeds and occasionally line up in formation and fly off into space."

Nearly every one of more than 50 police and sheriff's officers on the road between 12:20 A.M. and 2:30 A.M. called in to report seeing the objects.

The police officers, who had witnessed the flight patterns of the UFO's, weren't about to accept any official debunking.

"We saw three different objects," a patrolman reported. "They looked like white stars with green and red flashing lights. One stopped dead overhead for about 20 minutes, then took off in a northeasterly direction, moving at a terrific rate of speed."

A Shorewood officer, grimly aware of the Air Force's official decree that the Minneapolis citizens were seeing "unusually bright stars," had called in with one of the evening's first sightings at about 12:30 A.M. "I hope you don't think I'm crazy," he told the dispatcher, "but I just got passed by a star."

Later, the officer made out a report that told of a brilliant, white, star-like object that had roared past his patrol car at a low altitude.

After seven straight nights of increasingly active saucer activity, the *Denver Post,* on August 9th, published a "UFO log."

5:50 P.M.—Bill Lamberton, 17, of 1266 University Blvd., driving home from work west on W. Mississippi Ave., watched a silver object hovering in the air which looked at first like a cylinder, then flew up in the sky and disappeared west over the mountains." Lamberton observed it for six or seven seconds, as did two passengers in his car.

9:15 P.M.—Randy Holmes, 16, of 6120 Everett St. . . . reported sighting a "bright, yellow cigar-shaped object going along the horizon. It vanished completely to the northeast."

9:55 P.M.—Don Storres, 81 Greenwood Blvd., Adams County, said, "It was coming from the north at a very high rate of speed and going straight south. It covered three-fourths of the sky in just a few seconds and disappeared in a bright, red glow."

10:05 P.M.—Mrs. Lawrence Ausdahl said: "We picked up a UFO with our binoculars. At first it went to the right and after a while came back very fast and stood there for a few minutes. It appeared to be a dome-shaped object with red and green lights on its edge, like headlights on a car, and very luminous."

10:10 P.M.—Barbara Fisher, 2915 Yost St., "There were three lights, and the first two appeared to be going faster than the third. They were going from north to south in the vicinity of Buckley Field. . . . "

10:25 P.M.—Dan Terkins, 6602 Independence St. "It was a cone-shaped object with a dome on top of it and lights changing from yellow to red to green."

10:30 P.M.—C. I. Speaks, 8220 Tennyson St. "My wife and I and our neighbors saw a light streak by the North

Star and disappear over the mountains toward Boulder."

11:00 P.M.—Mrs. William McCall, 1620 Umatilla St., said that she and her two daughters saw "three dots which looked red at first and were close together. Then they separated and circled over the city from southwest to southeast. There was no sound of an engine."

Vaughan Aandahl, a George Washington High School math teacher, was in the habit of taking a few laps around the track before retiring for the evening. At 11:50 P.M., Aandhal was startled to see "a very large, white, luminous object flash through an open space in the clouds over south Denver.

"It curved in its path as it crossed the open space. It made a definite arc. There was no noise at all. It moved at tremendous speed."

Aandahl was certain that it had not been any known aircraft. "It was considerably larger than any commercial aircraft—more like the size of the football field that I was running around."

A duty officer at the North American Air Defense Command's space detection and tracking center at Colorado Springs told the *Denver Post* that he could offer no explanations for the sightings. "We're not in the UFO-type business," he said. Then, in his official capacity, he felt compelled to add that the big silver balloon known as the Echo 2 satellite would have been visible moving from northeast to north across the horizon.

On August 6th, some of the saucers had left their Rocky Mountain playground for the flatlands of Iowa. Police officers and residents in Washington, Muscatine, Clinton, Centerville, and Iowa City filed reports of having seen strange objects in the sky. Most of the Iowans reported a continuous bright light that changed color from blue to orange and took about three minutes to pass overhead.

Three 16-year-old Ames boys said that they had seen a UFO moving across the sky in a westerly direction. As they watched, the object had stopped, changed direction, and then went due north before fading out in the distance.

John Johnson of Iowa City filed a report of a sighting that he had made from his home-made observation post on the local golf course. He stated that the UFO had come up from the southern horizon, passed near the North Star before veering sharply off to the northeast and disappearing.

Although the majority of sightings of 1965's busy saucer summer seemed to occur in either North or South America, the European continent was not without its dramatic UFO incident.

On August 9th, gendarmes in the mountain village of Valensole, France were investigating a report made by a farmer who said that he had seen a mysterious aircraft take off from his field.

"It looked like a big Rugby ball and had four metal legs," Maurice Masse, 41, told the local authorities. "I discovered the craft at dawn. With it, was a small human form, about the size of an eight-year-old child.

"Suddenly the craft took off and disappeared in the sky. I couldn't believe my eyes."

M. Masse has a solid reputation in the mountain village for being a calm and solid citizen. A gendarme substantiated Masse's story by telling newsmen that he had seen strange tracks that the alien being and his spacecraft had left in the farmer's lavender field. "We don't think it was a gag," the gendarme told the press.

Hardly any thinking man considers UFO's as merely a "gag" in 1966, but nearly everyone continues to be confused by the conflicting reports issued by the Pentagon, the professional astronomers and trained observers, and the thousands of eye-witnesses to saucer activity. The Alameda, California *Times Star* echoed the sentiments of millions of bewildered Americans when it said: "It would surprise almost no one to learn that some UFO's are space-craft from elsewhere in the solar system or beyond. In fact, it would be even more surprising to learn that they were not. Hence, the only way in which the public interest can be served in this matter is for the Government to disclose what it knows about these phenomena."

8.

The Terrible Flying Jelly Bags

A report made by two young men is the strangest of all the cases in the archives of the Swedish Defense Staff. According to Hans Gustafsson and Stig Rydberg, nightmarish creatures from a flying saucer attacked them and tried to kidnap them on the morning of December 20, 1958.

Fantastic as the story sounds, two psychologists, who conducted extensive tests with the young men while they were under hypnosis, concluded that the two Swedes were telling what they considered to be the truth and that their story rested on an actual occurrence.

Detailed accounts of the alien attempt at kidnapping were carried in more than 70 European papers, including the *Svenska Dagbladet, Stockholf Tidnigen, Helsingborg Dagblad,* and the Swiss *Weltaumbote*.

A thick mist had slowed their speed to about 25 miles-per-hour that morning as they drove to Helsingborg from Hoganas. Just before 3:00 A.M., they had come to a clearing in the thick forest that lined both sides of the highway. It was there that they saw the mysterious light.

For all the ridicule and mental anguish to which they would later be subjected—not to mention a most horrifying experience—the two young Swedes have often wished that they had kept on driving.

But they did not. They felt compelled to investigate. They left their car and walked cautiously into the mist.

"We saw a strange disc," Hans Gustafsson told reporters and officials. "It was resting on legs about two feet

53

long. It seemed to be made of a peculiar, shimmering light that changed color."

The men had had barely time to express their amazement when they were suddenly confronted by a number of "blobs." According to Hans and Stig, "they were like protozoa, just a bit darker than the most, sort of a bluish color, hopping and jumping around the saucer like globs of animated jelly."

Before the Swedes had time to react to the creatures, the jelly-bags were enveloping them and, with powerful suction-like force, were trying to pull them towards the saucer.

"The drag the things exerted was terrific," the men said later. "And they gave off such a terrible smell—like ether and burnt sausage."

Stig Rydberg told investigators that his right arm sank up to the elbow in one of the blobs. "It almost seemed as if the creatures could read my mind. They parried every move before I made it. Their strength was not so great as the technique with which they wielded it."

After several desperate moments of frantic struggle, Rydberg freed himself from the sucking jelly-bags and ran for the car, with two of the pulsating globs in close pursuit. Flinging open the door, he slammed his arm against the car horn in the desperate hope that someone might hear the blare and come to their rescue.

The two young Swedes were saved by the horn.

The harsh blare that cut into the early morning mist seemed to have the effect of the sound of a rescuing cavalry's bugle on the quivering jelly-bags. Dropping Hans Gustafsson, whom they had stretched out horizontally as he clung tenaciously to a fence post, the protoplasmic creatures quickly retreated to the shimmering saucer and soared into the sky.

"As it shot upwards," the beleaguered companions noted, "it emitted a brilliant light and a piercing, high-pitched whistle."

Nearly exhausted with the incredible donnybrook in which they had just engaged, the two Swedes continued on their journey, each agreeing that they should keep the story to themselves.

"We knew that people would only laugh at us if we were to tell them this fantastic story," the men said later. "And the authorities would probably have us committed to an asylum. Besides, such publicity wouldn't do either of us any good."

But that terrible stench seemed to stay with Hans and Sitg. It seemed to have scarred their nostrils with its terrible odor. And their insides felt as though they had been turned upside down.

"We endured it for three days," Hans told newsmen, "then we decided that we should see a physician. We were afraid that those monsters might have permanently damaged us in some way, perhaps internally."

The doctor, after a careful and puzzled examination of the two men, told them that he could find nothing wrong with either of them. But the horrid, piping whistle still vibrated in their ears, and they still seemed fouled by the vile scent that had been exuded by the grasping blobs. At last they decided to make a public statement of their experience and face up to the mockery and undesirable publicity which they knew was certain to follow such a declaration.

For twelve hours, Stig and Hans were questioned and examined by officials from the Swedish Defense Staff, psychologists, doctors, and police. The multiple barrage of questions was unable to find the young men in a single contradiction or inconsistency. They made an offer—which was quickly accepted—to take the experts and the press to the spot where they had seen the saucer and its nightmarish crew. There, still visible, were the indentations which the space vehicle's landing tripod had made in the soft soil of the clearing. The psychologists concluded that their examination, conducted under deep hypnosis, had indicated that the two companions had definitely been caught in some mysterious magnetic field.

Danish officials were allowed to participate in the interrogation of Hans and Stig when they declared that Denmark's files contained a similar harrowing experience that had been endured by a Danish lady.

Neither young man had believed in "wild stories about flying saucers" before they stopped to investigate that mysterious light in the clearing. Neither of them will ever doubt such tales again.

9.

The Clergyman Who Waved Hello

The Reverend William Booth Gill, who has been the staff of the Anglican Mission in Papua, New Guinea for 13 years, had always considered reports of UFO's to be simply "figments of the imagination or some electrical phenomenon." However, in June of 1959, the clergyman filed a report consisting of eight closely typed pages, which told of lengthy saucer sightings that had occurred near his mission on the 21st, 26th, 27th, and 28th of that month.

Father Gill was quoted in the Sydney *Sun-Herald* as saying that he and 37 other witnesses watched UFO's for four hours on the evening of the 26th just after sunset.

"Four figures appeared on top of the large object, which seemed to be a mother ship. The figures looked as though they were doing something on the top deck. One figure seemed to be standing, looking down at us. I stretched my hand above my head and waved. To our surprise, the figure did the same."

The strange vehicle with the friendly aliens dropped down to an altitude of "maybe 450 feet, perhaps less, maybe 300 feet." Father Gill noted that a shaft of blue light emanated from the center of the deck of the UFO and would switch on and off every few seconds. According to the clergyman, "the craft looked like a disc with a smaller round super-structure, then again on top of that another kind of superstructure—round rather like the bridge of a boat. Underneath it had four legs in pairs pointing downward diagonally. These appeared to be fixed, not retractable, and looked the same on successive nights."

In a further effort to establish contact with the aliens,

a teacher named Ananias waved both his arms above his head and was delighted to see two figures return his greeting in the identical manner. Father Gill joined the teacher in the two-armed wave, and all four figures aboard the UFO responded in a like fashion. "There was no doubt that movement made by arms was answered by the figures," Father Gill told the *Sun-Herald* and emphasized in his personal report.

The natives at the mission were thrilled with the prospect of receiving such unusual guests, and they began beckoning and calling to the figures on the spacecraft to join them on the ground. The aliens made no audible response to the cheers and shouts of the mission natives, and Father Gill said that he could perceive no expressions on the faces of the men. "They were," he stated, "rather like players on a football field at night."

In a determined attempt to persuade them to land, one of the mission's teachers began to flash and wave a torchlight at the UFO crew. "It swung like a pendulum," Father Gill said, "presumably in recognition . . . it hovered, came quite close towards the ground . . . and we actually thought it was going to land, but it did not. We were very disappointed about that."

Although professing that he was "a poor mathematician," the Anglican priest estimated that the size of the craft was about 35 feet in diameter across the bottom deck and 20 feet across the upper deck. The color of the saucer was yellowish when stationary, but changed to a blue-green when in motion.

The calm and systematic Father Gill had all witnesses sign his report as testimony to the veracity of the account. The inhabitants of the Anglican mission agree strongly with Father Gill that "there is no doubt whatever that they (the UFO's) are handled by beings of some kind."

10.

Outer Space Tourists Are Messy, Too

Is there a connection between the strange droppings of wispy angel's hair-like substances and UFO's? Many observers seem to think so.

In January, 1966, I sat in the workshop-study of Ivan T. Sanderson and studied an acquisition of the famous natural scientist's newly organized Foundation. In a glass jar were some peculiar metal shavings, in appearance not greatly unlike the "icicles" one hangs on his Christmas tree. According to the young saucer buff, who had brought the jar for our examination, the shavings had been appearing almost nightly in one particular spot in the New Jersey area. How the metal residue materialized and who or what brought the shavings were unknown. At the time, samples of the metal were being analyzed by a laboratory in an attempt to determine, at least, from what kind of metal the shavings had come.

In February of 1958, the Miami *Herald* printed a story about a police detective who had reported a strange, white ball that had dropped into his back yard.

Detective Faustin Gallegos told a reporter that the body of the ball seemed to be made up of thousands of minute cells resembling those of a honeycomb. "It was not white as it had appeared when it fell, but was clear like glass. Amazingly, this translucent object was pulsating over its entire body."

Silencing powerful inner objections, as well as those of his wife, Detective Gallegos at last bent over to touch the pulsating ball. He was amazed to discover that he was "unable to feel it."

He got down on his hands and knees in an attempt

to detect an odor. He gingerly put forth his forefinger to once again touch the object. "Again I had no sensation of touch, but my finger gouged a furrow its entire length. I noticed that nothing clung to my finger—it was as if what I saw before my eyes actually wasn't there."

Detective Gallegos noticed that even the object was rapidly shrinking in size. In order to preserve some of the substance for the experts to examine, he quickly scooped up the still pulsating stuff into an empty pickle jar. By the time Gallegos arrived at the police laboratory to deliver the jar for analysis, however, it contained nothing which would indicate that anything other than pickles had ever been kept in it.

People who try to catch and retain drifting globs of "angel's hair" experience a similar difficulty in preserving the mysterious substance, which, according to those who have witnessed falls of the wispy material, seems to evaporate in the hand.

Mrs. W. J. Daily of Puente, California phoned the Mt. Wilson Observatory on February 1, 1954, seeking advice on how to best collect a specimen of "saucer exhaust."

Mrs. Daily had just experienced an UFO sighting when she was astonished to note a shiny, cobweb-like material flow out of the reddish colored saucer. The substance drifted down to earth and draped itself over trees, bushes, and telephone wires. According to Mrs. Daily: "It was long, silvery, like spider webs. But it vanished when I tried to touch it with my hands."

Equally as common as the sighting of the strange "angel's hair," is the discovery of a peculiar foam-like substance associated with UFO's.

On the morning of December 12, 1963, Customs Interventor Ignacio Gonzales Baz reported sighting and photographing two ball-shaped globs of foamy material which had bounced past the checking station and caught in the mesquite. The strange chunks of fluff were roughly six feet in diameter, and at first Baz had thought that they must be a concentration of soap or detergent suds that had somehow escaped the confines of a laundry.

Upon closer examination, however, Baz noticed that

the tiny bubbles seemed to be interlocked by a fibrous substance. The stuff clung cohesively together and stuck to the mesquite like large puffs of sticky cotton candy. Soap suds would, of course, have been instantly disintegrated by the rough contact of having been bounced into several rocks and mesquite branches before becoming caught fast. A rain storm dissolved the mysterious substance before it could be analyzed, but Baz's two pictures of the strange foam-balls appeared in an issue of the Douglas, Texas *Gazette*.

On November 16, 1953, such a large quantity of "angel's hair" fell in the San Fernando Valley that a bakery truck became completely enveloped in the wispy stuff. Two city blocks literally received a "blizzard" of the unearthly substance.

"It looked like finely shredded wool or spun glass," a resident was quoted. "But held between the fingers, it dissolves into nothing."

In October of 1952, over 100 citizens of Gaillac, France reported the formation of 16 flying saucers, which surrounded a large, cigar-shaped object. According to news accounts: "This object discharged a substance described as a bright, whitish filament, like glass wool." The material was seen to float down to treetops and telegraph wires and "many eyewitnesses gathered whole tufts of it. Unfortunately it disintegrated and disappeared before it could be taken to a laboratory for analysis."

If only, some day, a co-operative UFO would discharge some of this residue near a convenient chemical laboratory, a clue might be found to either the alien's fuel supply or their garbage.

11.

Helmeted Aliens Over New Zealand

At 5:30 A.M. on July 13, 1959, Mrs. Frederick Moreland was crossing the barn yard on her way to milk the cows. The Morelands enjoy country living and the nine-acre farm which they maintain on Old Renwick Road in Blenheim, Marlborough, New Zealand, suits them just fine. Mr. Moreland is a civilian employee at the Woodbourne Station of the Royal New Zealand Air Force, and on weekends, Mrs. Moreland is a nurse's aid at the Lister Hospital.

Mrs. Moreland was sleepily going about her early morning chores when she noticed a green glow in the clouds. As she told local police and a reporter for the Nelson *Evening Mail*: ". . . there was no moon so I wondered what it was. When I was half way across the paddock, two large green things, like eyes or big lamps, appeared above me and dropped towards the ground.

"I noticed that I was bathed in a green light and that the paddock was green, too. It was a horrid sort of color. My first thought was, 'I shouldn't be here,' and made a dive for the trees (a stand of pine on the other side of the paddock). There I stood watching.

"A saucer-shaped glow with two indented green lights in the bottom descended. The air became very warm. Two rows of jets around the middle shot out orange-colored flames. They appeared to revolve in opposite directions. The thing was about 20 to 30 feet in diameter. It hovered at about roof height.

"The jets stopped and a light was switched on in what appeared to be a . . . glass roof or dome, which glowed.

62

The bottom appeared to be of a grayish metal color. There was a faint hum in the air as it hovered."

Mrs. Moreland's early morning marvels had not yet ceased as she noted next that "there were two men in it, dressed in fairly close fitting suits of shiny material. The only thing I can think of to describe it is aluminum foil. Opaque helmets rose from their shoulders. I could not see their faces.

"One of the men stood up and put two hands in front of him as if leaning to look downwards. He then sat down, and after a minute or two, the jets started off again and, tilting slightly at first, the thing shot up vertically at great speed and disappeared into the clouds. When it did this, it made a soft but high-pitched sound."

Understandingly, Mrs. Moreland admitted to local authorities that her experience had left her "dumb-founded for a moment." As she stood in the trees to regain her mental equilibrium, she noticed the "smell of something which resembled pepper in the air."

With feminine logic, Mrs. Moreland continued about her chores and finished milking the cows before she went into the house to awaken her husband, who had worked a late shift at the Air Force Station the previous night. At his insistence, she phoned the local constable and the local press. Within a week, she was re-telling her story for an investigating officer of the New Zealand Air Force.

UFO investigators have often puzzled over the fact that so many sightings occur in Australia, New Zealand, New Guinea and the Antarctic, and that so many of these same sightings include prolonged visual contact wtih the alien beings that pilot the UFO's. The aliens may relax their security when they are "down-under" because they are aware of the communications lag between that area and the rest of the world. Never have aliens remained in view for longer than the four-hour period recorded by Father Gill and his mission at Papua, New Guinea. Imagine the furor such an incident would cause if it were to occur over New York City, London, or Moscow. Air-raid sirens would blare and rocket-armed jets would be sent in pursuit.

Jacques Vallee, French-born consultant on NASA's "Mars Map" project, commented on such backward area sightings in his *Anatomy of a Phenomena:* "The few cases when direct contact with men is said to have been made (i.e. gestures from a distance of a few meters) were associated with deserted areas, or, at least, very retrograde regions of France, Great Britain, Italy, the United States and South America . . . Landings made in populated areas were of extremely short duration."

If the saucer crews are intelligent enough to pilot their craft through several million miles of space, we may safely assume that they have technical data processing machines that would advise them that New Guinea, with one of the poorest communications systems in the world, would be a good place to "change a flat tire."

12.

So Why Don't They Visit Washington?

Six Army Signal Corps engineers looked out of the windows of their offices in downtown Washington, D.C. at the behest of one of their group who had observed some strange spots in the sky. It was 4:20 P.M. on January 11, 1965. The offices were located in the Munitions Building, and the engineers had a chance to observe the spots, which were reflecting the low afternoon sun, long enough to agree on the number and approximate shape of the objects and to estimate their altitude at between 12,000 and 15,000 feet.

As the engineers watched, the discs zig-zagged easily across the sky toward the capitol building, moving from north to south. Suddenly two delta wing jets burst onto the scene and began chasing the discs, but the objects outran their pursuers, seemingly without effort. Two of the engineers, Paul M. Dickey and Ed Shad, reported seeing a commercial airliner make a regular approach to the National Airport in about the same area of the sky.

The incident was one of many reported around the nation's capital in January of 1965. The press, eager for a statement or an explanation of the discs and the presence of the two jet pursuit planes in the area, tried to squeeze a statement out of the Defense Department. The official reaction was: "There was no such incident. It just didn't happen."

As if regimented by some unspoken law, officials of the military installation around Washington gave exactly the same reply to reporter's inquiries.

This unyielding position prompted one newspaper in the Washington area to run the headline, "PENTAGON

CAN'T SEE SPOTS IN SKY," over the story of the incident.

This was not the first time the UFO's had visited Washington. A wave of sightings in 1952 caused the biggest press conference since the Second World War. But just as in the early Fifties, the rare official who did comment on the 1964-65 sightings blamed them on meteorological illusions, wild imaginations, and the like.

But the presence on a radar screen of a solid object moving at speeds greater than any known jet, requires a more sophisticated explanation.

The first sighting officially occurred on December 29, 1964, but some independent investigators have speculated that the actual radar sighting took place ten days before but only leaked out to the public at the later date.

Three objects were detected by the radar screens. First one alone, then two together, all traveling at an estimated speed of 4,800 miles an hour. Weeks after the sighting had taken place, official Air Force sources blamed defective equipment for the presence of the objects on the radar screen.

In the countryside surrounding Washington, sightings of UFO's occurred both before and after reports were made in the city itself. Horace Burns, a gunsmith of Grottoes, Virginia reported a fantastic experience on December 21, 1964.

While driving along U.S. highway 250 between Staunton and Waynesboro, he was startled to see a huge cone-shaped object float into view. It glided across the road in front of him, and at one time, the outline of its shape more than filled the windshield in front of him. Without any warning of engine trouble, he said he felt "some sort of force" that caused his car to stop.

The strange looking craft settled easily in a meadow about a hundred yards from the highway as Burns climbed out of his stalled car. The gunsmith counted six concentric circular rings that diminished in diameter toward the top of the cone-shaped object. The top was crested with a dome, and the entire object emitted a bluish glow.

He watched the craft for a period of time which he

estimated to be a minute and a half. Then the craft took off at a "square angle," building up great speed instantaneously. Burns estimated the size of the UFO to be 75 feet high and about 125 feet at the base. It had no observable openings or seams.

Although the Air Force did not bother to make an immediate investigation, Ernest Gehman, a professor at Eastern Mennonite college, was curious enough to do a little investigating on his own. Taking a geiger counter to the reported place of landing, he found the radiation concentration at about 60,000 counts per minute. With the use of his geiger counter, the professor could trace the outline of the landing spot, and it checked with Burns' original estimation of the size of the craft. Two Dupont engineers checked the area and found that their readings agreed with Gehman's.

Over three weeks after the reported landing, the Air Force condescended to investigate the case. By that time, the area had been subjected to rain, snow, and the trampling feet of many curiosity seekers. The official opinion finally released was that the sightings were mirages.

The "mirages" were not content with a single manifestation however. On January 23, 1965, two men traveling on U.S. Highway 60 near Williamsburg reported that they had sighted a hovering cone-shaped object. Although the men were in separate cars and were traveling in different directions, both their cars had stopped as they had approached the object.

One report described the object as aluminum colored and cone-shaped. It had hovered over a cornfield next to the stalled motorist for 20 or 30 seconds before it vanished straight up into the air.

The driver traveling the opposite direction on U.S. 60 described a similar object likening it to an inverted ice cream cone. He estimated the height at 75 feet and described a "swishing" sound that he heard when he stepped out of his car. As in the first sighting, the object had disappeared straight upward at a great velocity.

Dempsey Bruton, chief of Satellite Tracking on NASA's Wallops Island, Virginia base, was standing in front of his house on January 5, 1965, waiting for the appearance of an artificial earth satellite, when a bright object appeared over the southwest horizon. It traveled at tremendous rate and gave off a yellowish-orange glow as it streaked through the sky. Several residents near the Wallops Island base confirmed Bruton's sighting by independently reporting it to the NASA installation.

Exactly one week later on January 12, a bright yellow-orange object streamed out of the sky and appeared to be heading right for a NASA public relations staff member. The light seemed to streak directly for the woman and her husband as they walked toward their house.

The NASA base had been the scene of even more UFO activity earlier. An incident in October, 1964 which had received little publicity was brought to light. Four men, three technicians and an engineer, observed a triangular-shaped object move over the base and execute a 90-degree turn. They all agreed that the object moved faster than any conventional jet aircraft and that the abrupt turn was impossible for an ordinary aircraft of any variety to execute.

A group of citizens of Marion, Virginia went on an excursion to investigate the reported sighting of a UFO on January 25. Woody Darnell, a Marion policeman, claimed that he and his family and several policemen watched a glowing object that hovered over them for several minutes before it took off in an explosion and a shower of sparks.

The group of investigators did not find the UFO, but they did find a number of trees that had had their tops bent over, and one green tree on fire in the area where the object had been reported. At Byrd Field, Virginia, TAC command officials had quickly come up with the explanation that the object was a plane equipped with a new arc light. Though this did not explain the fire, a thoughtful forestry official suggested that the "dead tree" had been set on fire by a hunter trying to claim a squirrel. These explanations were too far-fetched for anyone on the scene to consider.

Exactly twenty minutes after the Marion sighting, nine

persons near Fredricksburg, 275 miles from Marion, reported a UFO which they described as a "Christmas sparkler." It appeared to be spinning at a great velocity and spewing sparks from the bottom as it glided over the Rappahannock Valley.

On January 26th, the UFO's again visited Marion, but this time they were seen by many residents. Local radio stations and police were swamped with calls. All sightings were of similar fire-spewing or spark-shooting objects. Rev. H. Preston Robinson described a UFO that gave off a buzzing sound and had a round shaped bottom "from which several lights showed." The craft seemed to eject a ball of fire as they accelerated away from witnesses.

Perhaps the strangest story of all was that told by a Waynesboro, Virginia man, who described a scene right out of a science-fiction story. While chopping some wood at the August Archery range at Brands Flat on Tuesday, January 19, 1965, he noticed two bright objects in the sky above him. One was smaller than the other and proceeded to settle to the ground not more than fifty feet from him.

The man (who wished to remain unidentified) watched open-mouthed as an aperture appeared in what had seemed to be a completely smooth surface. Then three figures appeared and walked a few feet towards him. They appeared to be miniature humans with a reddish hue to their skins and eyes that seemed to drill holes in him. The entire procedure had occurred with very little sound, until the visitors made some unintelligible attempts at verbalization. Still holding the axe in his hand, the man stood transfixed, staring at the strange beings and at the craft they had come in. Finally the midget spacemen decided to leave, walked back into the ship, and resealed the entrance.

After the incident, the man wrote a description of the account and mailed it to himself, vowing to open it only if further sightings occurred. When reports of UFO's continued, the man revealed what he had seen.

13.

The UFO That Landed at a U.S. Air Force Base

If there is any one area in the world that consistently reports more UFO sightings than any other, it would unquestionably be the White Sands Proving Grounds in New Mexico.

Needless to say, the civilian population in the vicinity is more than a little uneasy about the frequency of the sightings.

Whether they admit it or not, so is the military. After all, it would be downright embarrassing, if not frightening, to admit that unconventional aircraft have penetrated the supposedly airtight blanket of security to the extent that they reportedly land near one of the most thoroughly instrumented bases in the United States. And it has been known since the early 1950's that UFO's can jam planes' radio frequencies and monitor transmissions. Uncomfortable proof of this allegation is the fact that the UFO's demonstratably know so much about our aerial procedures that they can simulate coded FAA recognition signals.

On April 30, 1964, local news media personnel were buzzing with the rumor that a UFO had been captured on the ground and was being kept in a Holloman Air Force base hangar under heavy guard.

Indefatigable saucer investigator Coral Lorenzen, author of *The Great Flying Saucer Hoax* and an international director of the Aerial Phenomena Research Organization, immediately followed through on the startling rumors by putting in a call to Terry Clarke of KALG Radio in Alamogordo, nine miles east of Holloman.

Clarke told Mrs. Lorenzen that his information source

had monitored the range radio communications that day. The essentials of that tape were published in an article by investigator Lorenzen in the October, 1964 issue of *Fate*.

"The loudspeaker at Main Control on the Holloman Air Force Base-White Sands Proving Ground Integrated Test Range suddenly blared these electrifying words: 'I've got a UFO.'

"It was Thursday, April 30, 1964. A lone B-57 was flying a routine mission in the vicinity of Stallion Site, a few miles east of San Antonio, N. Mex., on the north range . . .

"The controller then asked: 'What does it look like?'

"The B-57 pilot replied: 'It's egg-shaped and white.'

". . . minutes later, after the big jet had made its turn and come in over the area where the UFO was first seen, the pilot contacted Main Control again and reported: 'It's on the ground!' "

Then, according to Terry Clarke's information source, photo crews were asked to stand by just before radio communications ceased, and a major security clamp-down was put into effect.

Because of the stringent security measures applied, Mrs. Lorenzen was unable to learn to her complete satisfaction whether the pilot had been suffering from one of the standard Air Force "optical illusions" or whether the U.S.A.F. did indeed have a flying saucer secreted away in a hangar at Holloman. Subsequent investigation served only to reveal another story of a UFO on the ground, which had been discovered by a guard on the range at night. When the distraught soldier was returned to Base Headquarters, according to Mrs. Lorenzen's informant, he required sedation and hospitalization.

14.

The Saucer That Chased a Japanese Airliner

Yashika Inaba eased back on the throttle of the TOA Airlines Convair 240 he piloted as it taxied down the runway. It was the beginning of another routine flight. He carried 28 passengers on this March 18, 1965 flight, and after lift off, he and his co-pilot, Tetsu Umashima, went through routine checks of all the plane's systems before settling back to cruise along the sky ways.

At 7:00 P.M., an object appeared in the dark sky just after the plane had passed the small island of Himeji. Inaba checked his altimeter and found it registering the proper 6,000 feet, and he wondered what else was flying at that level. As the object approached, he found that it was nothing that was supposed to inhabit the airways of the earth.

His description had the object emitting a greenish color, and as it approached, it disrupted the normal operation of his automatic direction finder and cut off radio communication with the nearby landing fields.

During an inquiry about the event, Inaba testified: "I was flying at about 6,000 feet. The object followed for a while and then stopped for about three minutes, then followed along my left wing for about 55 miles until we reached Matsuyama in Shikoku. After this it disappeared."

Co-pilot Umashima tried several times to break the radio silence, but he could not contact any ground stations. On one of his calls, he did pick up the frantic voice of another pilot, Joji Negishi, who was himself flying a Tokyo lines small Cherokee 140. Negishi was also being followed by a strange luminous object as he flew along the northern edge of Matsuyama City.

This was of no help to the airliner, and the two men in the cockpit were concerned that the object might collide with them. Inaba made a 60-degree turn to the right, but the object, which was following closely on the right wing, did not fall back at all but stayed hovering close to the wing. Though the object did the airliner no harm, it followed astonishingly close to the plane and duplicated the maneuvers of the plane with ease.

After carefully considering the situation, officials investigating the case established that it was unlikely that the pilots were fooled by any meteorological phenomena. The sky was clear at the time of the sightings and the moon was full. An instantaneous illusion, perhaps one that had reflected off another plane was possible, but not one that hovered near a moving airline for more than fifty-five minutes. To further establish this fact, TOA Airline officials tested the pilots and the planes involved under almost identical conditions, and the results showed that neither the planes nor the pilots were in the proximity of any recurring natural phenomenon.

The object that Joji Negishi sighted followed his Piper Cherokee 140 very closely for a while before it vanished instantly. After it had disappeared, Negishi was able to make contact with the airliner piloted by Captain Inaba.

Four days after the incident, the *New York Times* Tokyo office reported that aviation, astronomical, and defense experts were arriving in Japan from the United States. These men were supposedly concerned with the mysterious air disasters that had been occurring over the Indian Sea between Japan and the mainland of the Asian continent. The possibility that such flying objects had been involved in the mishap was strongly considered.

On March 24, even more interest in the incident was stimulated when three men from the UFO Observer Corps arrived on the Japanese scene to talk to the witnesses. The international and semi-professional organization's meticulous investigation uncovered more sightings of UFO's that occured around the time the objects were chasing planes over the Inland Sea.

Passengers of a different airline reported that they had

sighted two shining, round, white objects as they flew over southern Hokkaido after taking off from the Chitose Airport enroute to Tokyo on March 18th.

What were these strange objects that filled the skies over Japan in March of 1965? One suggestion was that those were manifestations of the rare phenomena of balled lightning. This is highly unlikely, though, since the weather that usually produces such electrical phenomena is the electrically turbulent air that follows a thunderstorm. The weather condition at all of these sightings was perfectly clear. The specific identity of the UFO remains a mystery, while the sightings themselves form one more piece that does not fit in the puzzle of the airline crashes over the Inland Sea.

15.

The Paralyzing Force That Stalked an English Village

An army veteran, Major William Hill, of Warminister, England has headed for the weekly parade of the territorial army when at 8:22 P.M. the motor of his car stopped abruptly and the vehicle jerked to a stop. Although the car was in perfect running order, the lights flickered and the starter would not turn over the motor.

Muttering to himself, Bill Hill, who manages a big motor company garage, climbed out of his car to investigate. When his feet touched the ground he was hit by a force that rocked him on his heels. In an account carried by United Press International, he described air vibrations that seemed to surround him. He heard a sinister whining and crackling. "I sensed something fantastic and really menacing in the air above," he said. "It was in keeping with the sounds of high-powered refrigeration or deep-freeze units. But this was way, way above that level, magnified thousands of times. After three minutes things were back to normal. I pressed the starter button, my jalopy purred away perfectly—just as if it never had been abruptly halted in its tracks at high speed."

Hill's description fits in with a pattern of events that had been occurring around the village of Warminster for some time. The man insisted that: "There was a definite impression of something pressing down on me relentlessly. It there'd been a trench or ditch handy, I'd have jumped into it with pleasure and relief."

Other citizens of Warminster had described similar things happening to them. But along with this strange kind of force, that seemed to hammer down out of the sky, other things were occurring which were just as un-explainable.

Rev. P. Graham Phillips, the vicar of Heytesbury, a small community near Warminster, observed a strange object in the sky over south Warminster. His wife and three children all observed it, and the vicar described it: "It was a brightly glowing cigar-shaped object, and it remained in the sky for over 20 minutes."

Altogether, 17 people reported sighting the object from various parts of Warminster. Harold Horlock, a factory security guard, and his wife, Dora, described it as "twin, red hot pokers in the dark sky, separated by a black space and hanging downward."

The people of Warminster, England have been plagued by strange occurrences ever since Christmas day of 1964. Since then, a weird force has stalked the usually quiet town, and strange lights have been seen in the sky. They have termed whatever is causing the strange phenomena, "the Thing."

More than one observer has commented that there may be a connection between the sightings of UFO's in the sky overhead and the strange force which comes over individuals of the town. The UFO's were not seen before the force began "dropping" in on the town. The force is invariably described as descending from above. And other UFO's when passing overhead have been known to cause the motors of vehicles to stall, just as William Hill's did before he was hit with the mysterious force.

But whether the events are connected or not, both the sightings and the manifestations of the strange force continue to occur. A 19-year-old resident of Warminster, Eric Payne, was returning home after a date with his girl. Mist rose off the marshland to greet him.

"It was a Sunday. I neared Drayton's School. Just short of the apex of the bend, I heard a loud buzzing. It was not from telegraph wires. I'm not dead sure from which direction it came—it was overhead so quickly that it took me by surprise. As it hovered over me, it sent shivers up my spine.

"Imagine a giant tin can, filled with huge nuts and bolts,

being whirled and rattled above your head. That's how it struck me. Then something struck me in reality! I looked upward to see if it was a low-flying plane. I felt a rain of sharp, stinging blows on my head and cheeks. A wind tore at my hair and hurt my eyes, it was so fierce. My head and shoulders were pressed down, hard. I tried to fight off the invisible attacker. Just before it lashed down at me, I saw no aircraft in the sky, no plane lights or anything.

"For some time I staggered about in the road, then managed to sink to my knees on a grass verge at the roadside. The ground was wet, but that didn't worry me. All I badly wanted to do was rid myself of that choking, clutching 'Thing.' "

After the attack which lasted about three minutes, Eric ran for his home as fast as he could move. His mother told investigators: "He wouldn't tell us the whole story for several weeks after. Dad and I were worried stiff he was heading for a breakdown."

Alan Chapman, a 26-year-old blacksmith of the town, described a UFO he picked out with a pair of binoculars. "I was watching the sky and saw something very unusual flying at high altitude from northwest to southeast," he said. "There was no sound, although a plane made plenty as it went over shortly before. What first caught my attention was a red light flashing on and off. I got a closeup with my 10x50 binoculars, which gave me good magnification. An aircraft carries lights, but surely not so many as this thing. Apart from the blinking red glow, there were other white and bright lights on either side of it. They shone constantly. I counted six. I could not make out any distinct outline. It seemed to be flying sideways, so far as I could judge. Its speed was terrific, and it did not keep a straight ahead course at all. It crossed the whole sky, vanishing before dipping below the horizon, in about three minutes. I timed it with my watch."

Similar sightings and other strange occurrences prompted the townspeople to call emergency meetings. On August 28th, more than 600 of the citizens turned out for a public inquiry. Many suggested explanations were considered by the people, but none made much sense to those who had been victims of the forces or witnesses to UFO sightings. Some theorized that the sightings and other strange occurrences were the result of mass hysteria. Although it is difficult to say how people felt in private, public opinion sided with those who wrote off the "Thing" as a lot of malarky.

But some of the effects could not be denied by any intelligent observer. The UPI carried an account of Terry Simpson, a Westminster resident and truck driver.

"I was driving along Westbury Road in Warminster at 5:25 A.M. with a load of fruit," his account begins. "Then all of a sudden there was a close, blinding light just to my left. It was not a searchlight, I'll swear to that. It lit up my cab and blinded me for a split second. I had to jam on my brakes tight and skidded off the highway. I jumped out and got a good look at the light. It seemed to be a thing of substance. It was overhead and shaped like a ball. It was dancing about. There was no shaft of light beneath as you'd get from a searchlight's gleam. I kept looking until it suddenly went out—blew out like a candle—with funny, frizzling noises. It shook me up all right. I got the hell out of there."

At 1:55 A.M. on September 5th, some of the scoffers at the mass meeting were awakened by what they termed a "tremendous explosion." About 30 people, most of them men, described a 200-foot, orange-colored "mushroom" of smoke, with a glowing orange center. An orange light flooded the city, which in some sections changed "night into day." The explosion shattered many Warminster windows, and Bill Curtis, a resident used to hearing the firings from a nearby military range, said that he had never heard any artillery like it. "Our house was like a ship rocking in a big sea," Curtis said. Army officials could not explain the blast.

Lately all manner of strange happenings have been blamed on the weird force. Everything from the mysterious appearance of a spring-fed pool of water in someone's back yard to a thistle that grew to the height of 12 feet has found its explanation in "the Thing."

Although no one of any scientific repute has investigated the Warminster reports, many of the residents themselves feel that the force can only be caused by something from "outer space." In groping for an explanation for the dozens of mysterious happenings, many citizens agree with Mrs. Dora Horlock, who says of the 12-foot thistle that grew outside her cottage: "Something must have dropped out of the sky to make it grow so big."

16.

The Photographer and the Red Hot Saucer

"See you later, Papa," Edgar Schedelbauer said as he walked out the door of his aging father's house at Wildon, in the Leibnitz near the Yugoslav border of Austria.

The stooped figure of the old man hobbled to the doorway. "You take it easy, son," the figure said raising his finger. "I don't like to have you running around on that contraption so late at night."

"This?" Edgar thumped the seat of his motorcycle firmly. "It always gets me where I'm going."

"But at one-thirty in the morning you never know what you're going to meet between here and Vienna."

"Worry, worry, worry," Edgar said gently. "You go to bed. I've traveled this road many times. Nothing will happen."

"All right," the aging man conceded.

Schedelbauer kicked the starter twice before the engine caught, then he roared smoothly out of Wildon, moving toward the city and his job. He worked as a staff photographer on the *Wiener Montag,* a newspaper of Vienna, and he had a camera strapped over his shoulder as he powered his way over the early morning deserted roads of the Austrian countryside. The air was cool in the early morning of March 2, 1960, but the vibrating motorcycle under him gave him a feeling of power.

Shortly after he had left Labuttendorf, the usually uneventful trip became one which he would not forget for the rest of his life. In front of him, he perceived a large and brightly glowing object hovering over the forest. His motorcycle cruised toward it, and as he watched, the glowing thing crossed a clearing by the road. It then traced the outline of a semicircle as it drifted closer and closer to the ground.

Overcoming his initial astonishment, Schedelbauer let his motorcycle fall into the ditch as he jerked the camera over his head and loosened the leather case. He had no idea how long the inordinately bright object would remain hovering in the one spot, but he wanted a picture of it before it vanished from view.

Excitedly, he was able to snap the shutter once before the thing began to move again. The photographer later described it as looking like a "giant spider," and only after he had taken the picture did he notice the tremendous amount of heat the object was giving off. A low humming noise filled the early morning air as the object glided easily about.

Without warning, the sound changed from a low hum to a deafening roar. Schedelbauer said it reminded him of a jet. Then the UFO moved out of view in the direction of Radkersburg.

Schedelbauer raced to Vienna, praying that the picture which he had snapped of the object had been properly exposed. Taking pictures in the dark is tricky, even for a professional photographer, and he had barely had time to find the object in the camera's viewfinder before it powered out of sight. He developed the roll and found that indeed his camera had recorded the brighly glowing white object, although its movement had caused the outline to be fuzzy. The *Weiner Montag* published the photo together with the photographer's account.

Edgar Schedelbauer was not entirely ready for what followed the publishing of this sensational photograph and story. He became the immediate center of a lot of attention. Experts subjugated both him and his photograph to a close examination. But no matter how he was tested, he stuck to his story. "The camera is my witness. Besides I felt the heat. For three days great red spots showed on my face and hands, but they neither itched nor hurt."

His story was examined and re-examined. Vienna meteorological experts ruled out the possibility that the sighting was any normal natural phenomena, but skeptics viewed the photograph itself with a hypercritical eye.

More than one experienced photographer began an investigation, fully as skeptical as anyone else, but ended up confirming the validity of the photograph and calling it the most sensational snap of the century.

The consensus is that the photo was taken at about 1/50th of a second, a rather slow shutter speed for moving objects. Whatever it was that exposed the film was very bright and rotating at a fairly high velocity.

While the shutter was open, the object may have moved from five to fifteen feet or even more depending on the exact shutter speed that the photographer used. The blurry quality recorded on the film was due to the object's movement while the shutter was open. Several photographers feel that an adequate analysis of the picture will reveal the exact shape of the UFO and the approximate speed with which it traveled.

The professional eyes of these men confirmed that the object more likely was one of the "saucer-shaped craft" that have been seen at various places all over the world. They have determined the angle of climb of the craft and the fact that the object was rocking slightly as it moved upward during the exposure of the film.

Authorities considering all the evidence, from the opinion of professional photographers to Edgar Schedelbauer's experience, personality, and reputation, have come to the same decision that the editors on the *Wiener Montag* did when Schedelbauer first related the tale to them: the incident has to be taken seriously.

17.

The UFO That Sank in a River

Ruth de Souza, nine-year-old daughter of Senora Elidia Alves de Souza, was playing near the bank of the Peropava River when a loud roar frightened her and caused her to look up into the sky. What she saw coming at her was even more startling.

A shiny, disc-shaped object moved slowly just above tree top level. As it moved toward Mrs. Souza's house, it lost altitude and collided with a palm tree growing between the house and the river. Unable to move, the little girl watched awestruck as the shiny craft seemed to try to gain altitude as it moved over the water of the river. It rocked violently and maneuvered awkwardly for a while as if trying to regain stability. Then it suddenly dropped directly into the water of the river.

The nine-year-old ran to her mother, who had come out at the sound of the tremendous roar. Had there been no other effects besides the roar, the disc-shaped object that the little girl described might have been written off as the construction of a child's imagination. But when Mrs. Souza reached the river, the water where her daughter said the object had fallen was boiling violently, churning up mud and other debris from the bottom. Raul Alves de Souza, Ruth's uncle, who was working about a hundred yards away from the spot, came running to the house at the sound of the roar. As he looked out over the river, he, too, witnessed the strange boiling, churning water.

But even with these witnesses, Ruth's story might have gone unbelieved had not verification come from across the river. Fishermen working the opposite bank of the river described exactly the same phenomena that Ruth had. They all heard the roar and saw the craft as it moved over the river, then plunged into it.

It was 2:30 P.M., October 31, 1963 when the saucer fell. Senora de Souza's home is located in the Sao Paulo province of Brazil, and a report of the sighting and of the fall of the object immediately went to the city of Sao Paulo. Police from the nearest town, Iguape, went to the scene at once and questioned the witnesses while the incident was still fresh in their minds.

The story they pieced together described a disc of small thickness, about one meter (39.37 inches), but about five meters in diameter (16½ feet). By all accounts, it had resembled an "aluminum basin." It had been very bright, and in broad daylight it had looked almost luminous.

When first sighted, the craft was moving very slowly, and at no time did it show any ability to accelerate at any great rate. The roar that announced its coming was almost deafening and seemed to indicate that the craft possessed great power. As it moved toward the de Souza house, it appeared to be having difficulty maintaining its altitude. After several erratic movements, the power had seemed to give out, and the disc had plunged toward the river.

All the witnesses agreed that the river had erupted violently, and the water had begun to boil. The craft did not stay on top of the water for any time at all, but settled immediately beneath the surface, indicating that it was of a greater average density than water.

The depth of the water at the spot is 12 feet, but where the water stops the silt begins, and the mud layer on the bottom is about 15 feet thick and is mixed with clay.

The disc had struck the top of a palm tree next to Mrs. de Souza's house before it had moved over the river. The police observed that something had freshly gouged a chunk out of the tree about fifteen feet above the ground. Whatever the object's identity, it had been very substantial, heavier than water, and in trouble before it plunged into the river.

The incident caused an immediate sensation in Brazil. UFO investigators had waited for years for a saucer to land or crash in order to establish their claims to the existence of extra-terrestrial intelligence. This seemed to be the perfect opportunity. The craft had sunk in a river, but it had not fallen on military property. It seemed to be just a matter of recovering it where it had fallen.

The first attempt to retrieve the disc was made by a diving instructor, Caetano Germano Iovanne, with two companions, Peter Runger and Manoel Batista Andrade. They spent four hours searching the bottom in several efforts, but they were hampered by the mud. Although the exact spot of descent into the river was marked, exactly what had happened to the disc-shaped object once it had passed under the surface was a matter of speculation. One possibility is that it had sunk straight down into the mud and silt layers on the bottom. Yet, if it had not moved immediately into the mud, the current might have pushed the object toward the ocean. It also could have moved under its own power underwater before finally coming to rest on the river bottom.

Another attempt to recover the disc was made by a second team of divers led by a man named Gigi del Maschio. Although much special equipment was brought in by the determined group of men, they had as little luck as the first team. Once again the mud on the river bottom was the biggest obstacle to successful diving.

More than one try to find the disc has employed sensitive mine detectors and other probes, in the hope that such metal detectors could penetrate the veil mud coating the river bottom. Yet each attempt has gone unrewarded, and the mystery surrounding the disc that passed under the surface of the Peropava River has become as thick as the mud on the bottom.

Several theories concerning what happened to the disc have been advanced by the residents of Iguape and by the divers who have gone in search of the object. The most immediate possibility is that it may have been washed downstream. Most of the witnesses to the crash think that this is unlikely. The way the disc plunged into the river, it was probably a very heavy object.

Those believing that the disc had come from some point in outer space have suggested that it may have been secretly retrieved some night immediately following the crash. But eye-witnesses to the crash contest this position, pointing out that immediately after the craft hit the water, mud was spewed up which would indicate that it had probably buried itself deep in the silt, making such an operation extremely difficult. Furthermore, any mysterious activity in the alerted Iguape area surely would have been observed by the residents.

The remaining possibility, and the one which many people consider to be the most likely, is that the disc is still there! Perhaps it moved with the current underwater, or even under its own power, but it is probably buried somewhere between the banks of the Peropava, still settling to the bottom of the fifteen-foot layer of enveloping, almost impenetrable, mud.

With the reports of the witnesses and the evidence of a notched palm tree, the facts seemed to indicate that an unidentified flying disc had had navigational trouble over Brazil and had been forced down in the Peropava River. Whether it was manned or operated by remote control is unknown, but the witnesses agree that it seemed to be moving under its own power when it plunged into the water. It forms another mystery yet to be unraveled.

18.

First Cousin to a Lightning Ball?

On August 12, 1956, a Russian transport plane was flying through a slowly moving cold front in eastern Siberia. The plane was at an altitude of 11,000 feet at 12:45 P.M. when it entered a thick, rain-bearing cumulonimbus cloud.

Then, according to pilot Dubinski, co-pilot Sergienko, and navigator Fedayev, the crewmen saw a "rapidly approaching fireball 25 to 30 centimeters in diameter. It was dark red, almost orange. When it was less than a foot away from the nose of our plane, it swerved to the left and started to go around the running light. The fireball then collided with the blade of the left propeller, which was in its upper position, and exploded, causing a flaming band to move along the left side of the fuselage."

Although the force of the explosion caused the transport to be tossed about, the pilot swiftly regained control. Later, one of the aviators said that the blast had been a "blinding white flash with an explosion so loud that it could be heard over the noise of the engines. The radio operator suffered an electric shock when he attempted to disconnect the antenna."

After the plane had landed, maintenance crews discovered that the tip of a blade on the left propeller had been melted away.

Is it possible that many people, who claim to have seen UFO's, have in reality witnessed the chaotic flight pattern of one of the earth's more bizarre natural phenomenon? Ball-lighting, or fireballs, are formed during thunderstorms and are thought to be ionized pockets of air the molecules of which have massed together into super-hot balls of electro-magnetically glowing light.

Dr. Harold W. Lewis, professor of physics at the University of Wisconsin, has analyzed the sightings of several hundred lightning balls. "They usually materialize immediately after an ordinary lightning stroke," the physicist has said. "The ball can be almost any color, although green and violet are rare. Most seem to shine steadily, but some pulsate."

Although most specimens of ball-lightning have been harmless, some have scorched wood, burned through wires, and killed animals and humans with which they have come into contact. The *Bulletin of the Astronomical Society of France* carries an account of a 17-year-old French girl, who was touched and killed by ball-lightning when she took refuge from a thunderstorm in the doorway of a house. The deadly power of a fireball is understandable considering that the estimated temperatures of some lightning balls is 9,000 to 10,000 degrees Fahrenheit.

The phenomenon is, of course, simply an energy mass and not a malignant creature. Generally no harm comes to human beings because the majority of fireballs avoid conductors, as they are wafted about on air currents. A lightning ball with a high-current, however, would naturally attach itself to such a fine conductor of electricity as human flesh and cause severe burns or death.

The fireball is an eerie phenomenon to observe and the description given could easily fit many alleged UFO sightings. According to Dr. Walter Brand, a German physicist who completed an extensive survey of ball-lightning in 1923, "a hissing, humming, or fluttering noise is usually heard when the ball is nearby. They may disappear almost silently, with a mild crack, or with a blinding explosion."

Dr. Carl Benedicks, a former president of the Royal Swedish Academy of Science, has offered a theory which he feels may account for several sightings which have been credited to UFO's. Dr. Benedicks has stated that surface tension of the gases in the ball-lightning reflect light, which produces an illusion of a silvery metal appearance. The Swedish physicist goes on to theorize that, because a gas mass cooled by suction moves rapidly away from the direction of a cooling force, the lightning ball would appear to "fly away" from the aircraft that might attempt to "run it down."

19.

The Teen-Agers Who Were Pursued by a Saucer

The 1956 Ford Victoria moved easily out of the Kerasota Drive-in Theater at Mount Vernon, Illinois. Inside the car, Ronnie Austin and Phyllis Bruce, both of Fairfield, Illinois talked over the movie they had just seen, *The Great Escape.* It was about 11:30 P.M. of August 5, 1963.

Shortly after passing the Mount Vernon airport, traveling east on Route 15, the couple noticed a round ball of light just above treetop level in the southwest. Apparently the size of a washtub on first sighting, the couple watched the strange-looking, fuzzily-outlined ball, which to their surprise, seemed to be keeping pace with them as they moved over the pavement.

It was unlike an airplane of any variety, and it seemed to have no distinct outline. When Ronnie let up on the gas, the ball of light slowed, too. The fiery tail was becoming more than just a funny coincidence, it was becoming a disturbing fact, as the youth pushed the accelerator to the floor boards, calling on everything the souped-up Ford had. The car flew across the road, but the light kept pace with the rapidly moving vehicle, even at speeds up to 120 miles per hour.

The light remained gleaming over the right rear fender of the car for some time, until it suddenly swerved directly at the car and only stopped when it appeared to be a few hundred feet away. Then, just as suddenly, it swerved upward and perched momentarily over the top of an electronic relay tower. But it did not stay stationary for long. As it left its post and darted across the road, it ended up about two hundred yards in front of the car, where it bobbed like a frantic rabbit in a greyhound race.

Shortly after it had assumed this position, Ronnie turned the 1956 Ford off the paving and onto the gravel road that led to his date's house. The light stayed right with them for the full mile and half to her house. When Ronnie stopped the car, the light stopped also and stayed motionless in the southeastern sky. The couple watched it from the Bruce home for about 15 minutes.

As the car pulled out of the Bruce driveway, the light began to move again, until it had resumed the now familiar position in front of him. The car retraced its path for about a mile along the gravel road, but no matter how the young driver zigged or zagged, he could not shake the persistent light.

As the Ford turned east on another gravel road, a mile from the Bruce farm, the light began a variety of new antics. Ronnie Austin did not want to spend any more time in the company of the weird light than he had to and was moving at a high rate of speed when the light changed color. Its original dazzling white color had changed to a duller orange. After making the corner, the light darted straight for the speeding automobile, moving at a tremendous speed and did not alter its course until it was within 100 feet.

From this distance, the youth estimated the size of the light to be about the size of an automobile. Then the ball swerved away from its collision course and passed over the top of the car. At the same time, the car's radio erupted in a burst of static and the motor sputtered and almost died before the light moved back over a distant barn. As the light had approached, it had changed from a dull to a brilliant orange, but in the position that it had resumed in front of the car, it returned to the original dull orange color.

The car hurtled down the road toward the Austin farm, and terror seized the youth in the summer darkness. For almost three miles it stayed on his right rear fender while he was traveling north over the gravel. When he turned west, the light cut across the road behind him and pursued him literally right up to his door.

Running out of the car, Ronnie awakened his family, and his mother, father, brother, and sister all looked at the mysterious light from their kitchen windows. It seemed fixed in the eastern sky above a darkened farmhouse about 200 yards from the Bruce home.

At 12:25 A.M., Mr. Austin decided to call County authorities and have them get in contact with the Air Force. These officials contacted Deputy Sheriff Harry Lee and told him to investigate the report. He was not the first to arrive on the scene, however, as State Trooper Richard Gidcumb of McLeansboro and George Sexton, Village Marshal of Wayne City, had intercepted the radio message and had stopped at the Austin farm at about 12:45 A.M. Wanting as much verification as they could get, the Austins also called their nearest neighbors, Mr. and Mrs. Dwight Withrow, who went outside and observed the light.

By the time Deputy Lee arrived at the Austin farm it was 1:10 A.M., and the light was fading away in the southeastern sky. Deputy Lee described what he saw as an extremely bright star which remained in the sky until dawn.

Ronnie Austin was visibly shaken when he arrived home. He could barely express himself. The Austins called Dr. S. W. Conarski, who prescribed a sedative, which the family had on hand, to help settle the youth's riled nerves. Deputy Lee had no doubt that the Austin boy had seen something that had thoroughly terrified him.

It was not long before the story made headlines. The *Chicago Tribune* gave it 15 column inches on its first page. Other newspapers picked it up, and soon the entire Midwest was buzzing with the news of the light that had chased Ronnie Austin across a twisting trail in southern Illinois.

Overnight, reports of sightings of other strange lights in the heavens came in from all over the Midwest. Around the town of Fairfield itself, keen eyes of the citizens turned to the heavens, hoping to catch a glimpse of whatever it was that had visited their community shortly before. Sightings of some strange heavenly phenomena became an almost nightly occurrence. A coming air show in Fairfield used the event as part of their advertising, appealing to people to come to Fairfield and have a chance to see visitors from outer space. The area had made saucer hunting a kind of festival activity.

To Ronnie Austin and the Austin family, the results were taken much more seriously. In the habit of going out every night, Ronnie was so shaken by the event that he did not stir from the Austin farm for several days. Plagued by reporters, investigators, and curiosity seekers since the sighting, the Austins found the aftermath far from pleasant.

Rigorous interrogation of the people who had seen the light left many doubts as to its exact nature. In the entire time it had pursued the car, Ronnie had not seen any kind of solid outline, only a kind of fuzzy brilliance. The night had been perfectly clear, and the night time temperature was an even 75 degrees. Although a few persons had reported some ground fog, Ronnie Austin said that he had seen none on his drive from Mount Vernon. Trooper Gidcumb, Marshal Sexton, and Deputy Lee all agreed that it was obvious that Ronnie had seen something, but they were emphatic in agreeing that the thing that they had been shown looked like an extremely bright star in the southeastern sky.

Exactly what it was that Ronnie Austin led on a highway speed chase over the back roads of Southern Illinoise is still a mystery. Several possibilities—all theorizing that the light was rooted in natural phenomena—have been suggested.

The brightest light in the heavens on August 5th, aside from the moon, was the planet Jupiter. And at about midnight, it was about 3 degrees above the horizon, a little south of east. Furthermore a distant object will appear to move parallel to a moving vehicle to an observer inside the vehicle.

Yet, if the light were simply Jupiter, how could it change positions from one side of the car to the other, or disappear in the southeast, since Jupiter sets in the west?

In some cases, light coming to the earth from stars

or the moon is bent and magnified by pockets of air which vary in temperature. This is the so-called mirage. Even if the weather bureau would not have ruled this out, it would not have accounted for the light's ability to follow the car over all sorts of terrain.

Another possibility is that the object was a lightning ball. Although this phenomenon is rare, the lightning ball is known to appear right after a rainstorm, in air which has been supercharged with static electricity. The weather around Fairfield had been hot and dry, and the night was clear.

One of the few remaining possibilities is that the light was extra-terrestrial.

20.

People Who Ride in Flying Saucers

Howard Menger not only successfully established contact with an alien, he married one. Or at least that is what Howard Menger said.

The complete flying saucer story cannot be told without digressing a bit to examine the claims of the "contactees," those individuals who profess an intimate relationship with alien UFO crews that extends to being invited on board space vehicles for inter-planetary flights.

"Saucer-hopping" was an immensely popular pastime in the early and mid-Fifties, and of all those courageous souls, who boldly accepted a quick trip to Venus and back, Howard Menger undoubtedly had the most romantic spiel—at least until he more or less took it all back.

According to Menger, back in 1932, when he was just a 10-year-old lad, he and his brother sighted a marvelous shining disc that landed in a nearby field. Being brave young fellows, they approached the glowing object and were greeted by an incredibly beautiful woman with long golden hair and golden flecks in her eyes. She was dressed in one of those form-fitting translucent jumpsuits that seemed to be standard dress for female space-travelers on all the old pulp science-fiction covers. As a healthy 10-year-old American boy, young Howard was able to notice that the beautiful golden lady truly had a form worth fitting. Although his conversation with the voluptuous alien was a brief one, Howard knew that he had fallen spiritually in love with her.

It wasn't until June of 1946 that the Venusians and Martians really began to pop up in Howard's life with any great amount of frequency, but once he had won their confidence, he did all that he could in the interests of inter-galactic peace and good will. He instructed the aliens in the use of American slang and briefed them on local customs so that they might blend into the citizenry and observe the natives at work and play without being noticed. In turn, Howard was invited aboard their space ships, taken along on brief junkets to the moon, and allowed to snap all the photographs that he wanted. The photographs, which were widely reproduced in saucer publications, were always rather dark, distorted, and blobby, and Menger apologized that he was such a poor photographer.

In addition to receiving instruction on matters celestial, Howard was taught to develop his own inner-occult talents, such as teleportation and astral projection. He learned that, in reality, he was a Saturnian, who had been reincarnated in the body of an earth baby named Howard Menger. He had assumed the role of Howard when the earth baby had died. He also learned, after catching a glimpse of a lovely girl named Marla Baxter, that she was the sister of the voluptuous golden lady. The beautiful Venusian, who was over 500 years old, told Menger that it was ordained that he and Marla should become man and wife. This was complicated just a bit by the fact that Howard was already married, but he couldn't let a little thing like a common, old earth-type spouse stand in the way of a cosmic union. He quickly divorced his wife, and Marla became the second Mrs. Menger.

Alyn (that was Howard's real Saturnian name) and Marla became very big on the saucer circuit in 1958. They had a number of artifacts, such as moon potatoes, to display along with their lecture, and, of course, Howard had written a book detailing his adventures with his Venusian and Martian comrades.

Howard Menger and his contemporary contactees (some of whom will be introduced a bit later) were simply capitalizing on the big saucer flaps of the early Fifties. Science had been expanding at a rate that was simply too rapid for the large masses of people. They were frightened that the malicious aliens and bug-eyed monsters of TV programs and science-fiction movies would soon become an inescapable reality. In addition to man's natural fear of the unknown, certain of the contactees saw a sure-fire way to profit from the widely-held hope that the flying saucers would bring within their domes superior extra-terrestrial beings, who were much wiser, kinder, and more generous than earthmen. With the saucers would come the end of wars, disease, and the sins of the flesh. A new Garden of Eden would blossom forth on this tired, old globe.

The saucer crews, according to the contactees, were always sublimely calm and wise. And they all had, without exception, a "message" for earthlings which one could obtain by purchasing the contactee's book.

To many people, the saucerians offered a key to the universe—a magic key which they felt had always been there, awaiting discovery.

The William Denton family of Wellesley, Massachusetts announced that they had been paying regular visits to Mars as early as 1866.

The Dentons were a family of practicing psychometrists, who believed in a spiritual universe. Their "trips," then, were strictly of spiritual nature, but, in many ways, their reports seem strangely prophetic today.

A psychometrist is one who "reads" the history of an object by psychic vibrations which he receives as he holds the thing in his hand. William Denton often said in his lectures that a personal relic of Shakespeare could, in half an hour, reveal more of the bard to one who had the gift of psychometry than biographers have been able to discover in 200 years.

"I have known a little dust from a copper knife to reveal the story of ancient copper-miners of Lake Superior," Denton said. "To the psychometer, the secrets of ancient times are as open as a field in the sunshine. We have only to open our spiritual eyes to discover them!"

Denton conducted many experiments with ancient relics and achieved some truly notable "impressions," which were subsequently proved to be correct.

In 1866, he became interested in using psychometry to bridge the great gaps between planets.

"A telescope," he said, "only enables us to see; but the spiritual faculties enable their possessors to hear, smell, taste, and feel, and become for the time being, almost inhabitants of the planet they are examining."

One evening after supper, Denton and his son, Sherman, were in the orchard. "Venus shone like a young moon in the western sky," Denton later wrote in one of his many volumes, "and I said to Sherman, 'look at that star; and then shut your eyes and tell me what you see.'

"Sherman described trees, animals that were half fish and half muskrat, and water that was heavy but not wet. This was the first of a number of experiments in outer space, achieved by choosing the object, then closing the eyes."

During another experiment, Sherman went "out into space" and reported that there were people on Mars who looked astonishingly like earth people. "They soar above traffic on individual fly-cycles," he told his father. "They seem particularly fond of air travel. As many as 30 people occupy some of the large flying conveyances."

On the Dentons' own planet, in the 1860's, aluminum had barely been heard of, yet the space-traveling psychometrists wrote that the Martians used it widely for building their homes, flying machines, and cooking utensils.

Denton's studies convinced him that the Martians had been examining our planet and had found us out as a people early in the 1800's. "I believe that we can in time learn to hold communication with them," he wrote. "Perhaps they are psychometers!"

The Dentons made a very comfortable living on the lecture circuit, giving demonstrations of their psychometric prowess and telling about life on other planets.

Each of the more imaginative contactees of our time has used the same pattern: establish contact with a superior alien culture, receive their particular secrets—secrets for which the "world" is not ready—then tell the world about those secrets for a reasonable fee. The contactee, unfortunately, has come to represent the sort of person who takes UFO's seriously in the minds of the Air Force, large sections of the scientific community, and the bulk of the citizenry.

Two positions of the contactee have always seemed particularly untenable. Why did the aliens seek out him, of all earth's inhabitants, as the one capable of receiving such high-powered information; and why, if the knowledge contained in this message was too potent to reveal to the Pentagon, the Parliament, or the Politburo, do the aliens allow the contactee to disseminate the message in cheaply printed, poorly written books and in speeches from the lecture platform? As for the contents of the celestial sermons, they can usually be boiled down to some occult-oriented philosophy mixed with equal parts of the "power of positive thinking."

It may not be difficult to believe that aliens have been observing this planet. And certainly one cannot shout "liar" at the clergyman in New Guinea, who said he observed them for four hours and communicated with them by arm signals, or the poor boy in Brazil, who claimed that they kidnapped his father, or the two young men, who were nearly sucked up inside a UFO outside of Helsingborg in South Sweden. But if the crews of the flying saucers truly are revealing their secrets to the contactees then one can not help questioning the aliens' choice of confidantes.

George Adamski certainly did not keep any cosmic secrets. His book on UFO's sold extremely well, and his lectures were always attended *en masse* by the UFOlogists and the curious.

Adamski met his spacemen on November 20, 1952. They, as all spacemen seem to be, were extremely handsome and beautifully proportioned and had recently arrived in a large, cigar-shaped saucer. Through his initial contacts, Firkon, a Martian, and Ramu, a Saturnian, Adamski met Orthon, a Venusian, and the inevitable Venusian beauty (it is inevitable that all contactees meet other-worldly females who make earth-women appear to be skinny boys by comparison.)

The fact that the space crews that Adamski communicated with were composed of a mixture of aliens from different planets indicated, of course, that earthlings are the only creatures in the universe capable of prejudice, crime, war, hate, and all the other planetary evils. Adamski got his ride in a flying saucer—50,000 miles above the earth—and received his secret philosophy to pass on to all who would buy a ticket to listen to his lecture or a copy of his book to read its esoteric contents.

Contacting aliens is definitely out of vogue in the Sixties. None of the momentous prophecies of the contactees have come to pass, but so many incredible things in the world of science have occurred in the past ten years that the majority of people have lost their naivete and are prepared to accept almost anything that can be properly demonstrated to their satisfaction. Curiosity about the ever-expanding universe has never been more active than it is among today's citizenry.

On the morning of April 24, 1964, however, Gary Wilcox, a 28-year-old farmer of Newark Valley, New York, claimed to have had a lengthy conversation with some "little men" who came in a flying saucer.

Wilcox had been out spreading manure when he was attracted to a nearby field by a bright flash of light. "A funny feeling came over me," he said later, "like something was going to happen."

An interviewer described Gary Wilcox as a "no-nonsense" man, who works hard and is intolerant of interruption to his farm routine. On this particular day, Wilcox was forced to tolerate the intrusion of an object in his field, which appeared to be about 20 feet long and 15 feet wide. He could hear a sound like "motor idling," but he just walked right up to the UFO and touched it.

His first reaction to the two little men who dropped to the ground from beneath the vehicle was that someone was playing a joke on him. Why he thought someone would spend the money to fashion a vehicle of such large proportions and employ two midgets to dress up in space outfits just to liven his manure spreading, Wilcox never makes clear. At any rate, the aliens told him not to be alarmed, so the farmer simply stood by and watched the humanoids go about their business of obtaining specimens of soil and sod.

When they began to question him about earthian farming procedures, Wilcox decided that it was no gag. He also decided to answer their questions politely and in a patient manner.

The aliens told the New York farmer that they had come from the planet Mars. Their mission was to seek methods by which the soil on Mars might be rehabilitated. They asked for a sample bag of commercial fertilizer that they might bring back to their planet with them.

Wilcox brooded about the incident for a couple of days before he reported the episode to the Tioga County Sheriff in Owego.

"I don't care whether anyone believes me or not," Wilcox said. "It doesn't mean anything to me one way or the other. I told them what I saw and heard. I thought I should."

Wilcox's brother, Floyd, stated that he believed his brother was telling the truth: "If Gary says this thing happened, it really happened. He has nothing to gain and a lot to lose by telling a story like this. I know it is true."

Floyd Wilcox did have a point there. His brother differed from the other contactees in that, to date, he has written no book or signed up for any lecture tours. And, other than making his report to the Sheriff, he has not done another thing to draw any more publicity of any sort to himself.

Surely, one must keep an open mind—skeptical, but open.

Again, one cannot help observing that it is only the contactees who describe the alien saucer crews as being humanoid. To the embattled Kentucky farmers at Kelly-Hopkinsville, the aliens were long-armed, floating monsters that proved invulnerable to their firearms. To the desperate Swedes, the aliens were horrid protoplasmic blobs that tried to envelop them.

Evolution, as human scientists see it, is a chancy affair. Although scientists generally agree that life must be fairly abundant in this and other galaxies, not all are confident that something like man has evolved elsewhere. The basics of life may well be the same in all parts of the universe, as there are good reasons for believing that carbon is the foundation element of life in the farthest as well as the nearest planetary systems.

But intelligent, man-like life may not necessarily be an inevitable product of evolution everywhere. It was not, for example, on our own planet. Nothing resembling man evolved in either North or South America or Australia. Man migrated to those continents but did not develop there. There may be thousands of planets, therefore, that may be rich in life but dominated by non-intelligent creatures, such as giant insects, that have the necessary "survival value" to evolve into planetary masters but which lack the cerebral machinery to trade messages with beings from other planets.

The beings that are capable of spanning the universe, whatever their physical shape, must be possessed of a high degree of technological sophistication of the kind possessed on earth only by beings who have mastered the techniques of extending their own limited senses into the electro-magnetic ranges of invisible radio waves, x-rays, and gamma rays.

Dr. Charles S. Sheldon II of the National Aeronautics and Space Council said recently that earth will have made its "first contacts with worlds outside" by the 22nd century.

It seems obvious to astronomers that there are habitable planets that formed, perhaps billions of years earlier than the earth, somewhere within a few thousand or a few billion light years from earth. If even one of these habitable planets developed on an evolutionary schedule similar to our own, it would seem quite possible to conclude that our "first contact with worlds outside" has already been achieved—by the "worlds outside."

21.

Portugal's Flying Cardinal's Hat

"I am accustomed to taking a quick look at Venus, which we call the 'morning star,'" said Mrs. Manuel Fernandez of Paico, Portugal, to a UPI reporter, "even if my husband says it is not a star but a planet."

Mrs. Fernandez was describing the early morning hours of July 12, 1965 in which she and her husband were witnesses to the strangest phenomena that they had ever seen in their lives.

"Well, I saw it as usual," her account continued. "Venus is like a good morning sign to me. If the sky is clouded and I don't see it, I feel sad. We country women can't help being a bit superstitious, even if the parish priest says we shouldn't.

"It was just then that I saw the thing. It was coming from the ocean, right from that direction at a very high speed," as she spoke she pointed in a northeasterly direction.

"At first I was not surprised at all, because I am accustomed to seeing planes take off or land all day long at the nearby Pedras Rubras Airport. There was a red glow about it, but since I know that planes have green and red lights on their wingtips, I was not impressed about that. But when it stopped in mid-air—*Valha-me Nossa Senhora!* (May our Madona help me!) I was really shocked because I know planes do not come to a halt in the sky.

"It was very red. It looked like a Cardinal's hat. I know, because once I saw our Cardinal in a religious ceremony at the Shrine of Fatima. He was not wearing it, but he kept it tied behind his back, tied with a red cord around his neck. Well, the thing was very similar

to Cardinal Cerejeira's hat, with a very large brim. It was
still in the air, hovering over the woods we have not too
far away from home. I dropped the buckets and rushed
back to warn my husband."

Manuel Fernandez was catching his sleep in the early
morning hours and his 200-pound wife had quite a time
arousing him. Fernandez works at a desk for the Trawler
Owners Association at Matosinhos, keeping records on
the number of tons of fish brought in daily by the fishing
fleet. As he stumbled out of bed, the radio at his bedside,
which had been playing softly, erupted in a violent burst
of noise. He found it hard to take his wife, who runs a
kindergarten for the neighborhood, seriously at first, but
the woman was insistent.

"Laura's (Mrs. Fernandez) story was so confused that
at first," said Manuel Fernandez, "I thought she had found
a Cardinal's hat in our courtyard. But high church dig-
nitaries usually do not have the habit of walking in our
courtyard and forgetting their hats there.

"I reckon the thing was about 400 meters (one-fourth
mile) distant from us. Just as my wife said, it looked like
a Cardinal's hat. It had a dark, round brim and a bril-
liantly-lighted, orange-colored round top, which gave us
the impression that it was lighted from the inside.

"At one point on the brim, exactly on the side closer
to the airport, there was a red, intensely-flickering light.
That 'thing,' which looked to me more or less like the
descriptions of flying saucers we have been reading about
in the papers for the last 20 years, appeared to be almost
still, just above the treetops. It was leaning alternatively
on either side very slightly.

"It's difficult to say how big it was," Fernandez said
later in the account. "It was still dark, though the night
seemed strangely clear. Maybe it was the result of that
orange light. I don't know. When I saw the thing, it was
still just over the treetops, and when I stretched my arms
out in front of me to get an idea of its size, there was
a distance of about 50 centimeters (about 20 inches) between my hands, each of them being pointed at an end
of the flying saucer. I imagine that at that distance, about

400 meters, it should have been a rather huge saucer, don't you think?

"We do not know how long the object stood there. I had left my wristwatch behind in the bedroom and, even if I had taken it with me, I was just too busy looking at that unbelievable thing. We think it remained over the woods for about three minutes after 4:30. Then it headed north at full speed. What surprised me most was its start, because it went off without any warning. There was no apparent acceleration before it moved northward. I mean it stayed over the treetops and suddenly was moving straight on—just like a bullet from a rifle muzzle.

"There is one thing that I didn't think was very important at the time. When the thing sped off to the north, the radio set in our room suddenly stopped making that horrible noise, and we could hear the music I had been listening to when Laura got me up. I can't help thinking that there may be a relation between the departure of the saucer and the fading away of the interference. It failed to impress me at the time because the saucer was speeding away before my eyes, and the radio noise was fading away behind my back. I went to Oporto last year and saw a motion picture where the sound seemed to reach the audience from all sides of the theater while we watched the picture. Well, it was like that."

The sighting over Paico, Portugal was not isolated by any means. Three days before, and a few hundred miles west of the little country in the Azores Islands, another UFO sighting was reported. The thing appeared drifting slowly over Santa Maria Island and was observed by many of the people on the Island. But shortly after the sighting, some of the most qualified witnesses refused to comment on the sighting, and the entire incident became clouded with an air of secrecy.

Aristides Arruda, a 31-year-old gardener at the Terra Nostra Hotel, was one of the witnesses. He first saw the object at 4:30 P.M. while cultivating a hotel flowerbed. He paused in his work and happened to gaze into the sky.

"It looked like a balloon to me," he related to newsmen for UPI. "Or at least that was my first thought, because it was moving so slowly that it seemed to be standing still. It followed a straight course from southeast to northwest, which was rather surprising because the wind was blowing in just the opposite direction. I turned around and saw that an American guest of the hotel also was looking at that thing."

Richard Godbold of New York was on the Azores, assigned to work at the radio facilities of Santa Maria. He worked for the U.S. Air Force Base at Lajes, Azores.

"Yes, I saw that thing," he said, "but since I am a radio expert I cannot give you a qualified opinion. It was certainly something, probably a balloon or even something else. Who knows? It was too high to judge it by the naked eye."

Angelo de Braga Chaves, a whale spotter from Marvao, had the opportunity to watch the floating object through binoculars.

"Seen through binoculars, it was almost like a cylinder floating vertically, but sometimes it was like a moon," Chaves says. "From the southwestern part of the island I got the impression that it was made of transparent plastic and contained something like two lamps. Anyway it was shining in the sun. I noticed that it moved against the wind or at least in a direction which was against the wind blowing at ground level. But that may mean nothing, because at that altitude the wind could be blowing in another direction."

From the witnesses' descriptions, the possibility that the object was a balloon could not be denied. But the most qualified observers of the thing, the airport officials, became extremely tight-lipped about the affair. If the object was a weather or observation balloon, why should an airport official refuse to identify it as such?

Antonio Francisco Pimentel da Cunha, a 28-year-old cab driver, was waiting for customers at the airport. "I stepped out of my cab when I heard people calling loudly to one another," he says. "I saw that thing, too. And since then I have listened to dozens of conflicting opinions about it. I have the impression that those who really know something are tight-lipped for reasons which a taxicab driver like me is certainly not able to guess. It could have been a balloon, or it could have been a flying saucer. But the more I think about it, the more I believe it was something unusual."

Another strange "coincidence" which occurred at the time was that the electro-magnetic clocks of the airport stopped functioning for ten minutes while the object was in the sky overhead. Though no official comments were made, some authorities suggested that there may have been a short in the clock circuit.

The identity of the object that was in the skies over the Azores remains a mystery. The witnesses will not buy the answer that it was a weather balloon since it floated into a cloud that was moving in the opposite direction and disappeared. Together with the "Cardinal's Hat" that flew over Portugal, it forms but another bit of drama in the great UFO mystery.

22.

Footprints and Footnotes in Florida

James W. Flynn, a well-known dog trainer and a highly respected resident of Fort Myers, Florida, was running some of his hounds through the swampy Everglades after dark on a mild March night in 1965.

As he plunged through the heavy swamp grasses, being careful to avoid foot-ensnarling roots, he could hear his dogs up ahead, whining and milling around. He frowned his bewilderment. If they had treed a raccoon, they would be baying and barking their excitement, not making high-pitched noises of fear and confusion.

Then, as Flynn burst into a clearing, he could only blink his eyes in astonishment as he saw his hounds noisily moving about a large, metallic cone-shaped machine. From four banks of portholes, a softly glowing light emanated.

The Floridian moved in closer to investigate the strange contraption that had landed in a clearing in the Everglades. The last thing that Flynn remembers about that night was receiving a "sledgehammer blow" on his head. When he staggered back to civilization that next morning, he was found to have suffered a mild concussion.

Because James Flynn was a highly respected citizen of Fort Myers, Florida, he fared much better than if he had been some "swamp-rat" who had come out of the Everglades with an aching skull and a story about a cone-shaped, glowing space machine in a swamp clearing. Flynn's story was investigated by intelligent and knowledgeable men, and they found a large, circular area fringed with burned underbrush and tree foliage in the spot where Flynn claimed to have seen the UFO.

March of 1965 was a busy month for aliens in Florida. On March 2nd, the wire services carried a story date-lined Weeki Wachee Springs that told of a Floridian who had had his picture taken by an outer-spaceman.

John Reeves is a 66-year-old retired New York City longshoreman, who lives alone in a small house at the site of his trailer court. Reeves likes to go for long walks in the open air and just think about things.

It was on one of these walks that he saw the UFO across the "flats." He had approached the machine slowly, using bushes for cover, being careful not to make a lot of noise.

He was within 150 feet of the disc-shaped thing when a "five-foot-tall being" stepped out from behind some bushes, just 100 feet away from him. Reeves froze, watching the creature move toward the machine. It was humanoid in appearance, Reeves remembered later for reporters, but "strange." Its entire body was clothed in canvas-like material of a silver-grey color, and it appeared to be wearing some kind of mittens. Non-oxygen breathing, the being wore a bowl-shaped helmet over a human-like face with extremely wide-set eyes and a very pointed chin.

Reeves got an even better look at the alien's physiognomy when the creature seemed to sense his presence and alter its course to get a better look at the earthling. It continued directly toward the frightened Reeves until it got about fifteen feet away. Then it reached into "its left side and brought out a black object six or seven inches in diameter."

When the alien raised the object to chin-level and began to sight through it, Reeves took out running. He had seen enough science-fiction movies to know that helmeted creatures from outer-space almost always carried deadly ray guns, and he had no intentions of being roasted in the Florida flatlands.

Before he had gone far, Reeves noticed that the object had flashed a brilliant light, and it suddenly occurred to him that he had just had his picture taken by a tourist from another world. The alien had advanced no further but simply stood still, observing the erratic flight of the frightened man. When Reeves paused, the creature flashed the object in his direction once again.

The last time that Reeves stopped to catch his breath, the alien had turned back toward the space ship. Then, according to the former longshoreman, the spaceman started up some stairs, which led into the underside of the saucer. When he had entered the machine, the cylinder containing the stairs withdrew into the bottom of the vehicle. A roaring sound became audible, which was shortly replaced by a high-pitched whistle. Within a matter of seconds, the UFO had blasted out of sight.

After he was reasonably certain that the flying saucer was not about to make a sudden reappearance, Reeves went back to the area to see if he might not find some evidence to make his story credible to others. He was pleased to note that the being had left a goodly number of footprints in the area and that the landing gear had made deep impressions in the soil.

While he was examining the figure-eight shaped footprints, Reeves came upon a tightly rolled-up sheaf of tissue-thin paper. Carefully unrolling the manuscript, Reeves was amazed to find two sheets of the filmy paper covered with strange, undecipherable marks.

The next day, Reeves went into Brooksville, told his story to members of the WFFB radio staff, delivered up the manuscript to personnel from MacDill Air Force Base, and returned with reporters and investigators to the spot where he had seen the alien and the saucer. News photographers snapped pictures of the strange footprints and the indentations made by the landing gear.

Reeves submitted to a polygraph (lie-detector) test, and the operator concluded that Reeves was not guilty of deception or of lying in giving the answers to the questions asked him in regard to seeing the UFO and the alien. Mr. E. J. Edwards, the polygraph examiner added: "A further and most significant point of interest is, at the conclusion of the tests, Mr. Reeves first remarked, 'Now, would you like to see the place where I saw the saucer?' The usual reaction of a guilty subject

with respect to not answering truthfully is more likely
to have been 'Well, how did I make out?' There was, in
Mr. Reeves, a complete unconcern about the polygraph
test outcome. It is my opinion, therefore, that he was
truth-telling in all respects."

Two months later, the Air Force returned the alleged
alien script with the charge that the whole thing was
an obvious hoax. According to Air Force investigators,
who had decoded the ciphers, the message read: "Planet
Mars—Are you coming home soon—We missing you
very much—Why did you stay away too long."

Reeves, confused and troubled by the Air Force's
charges, insisted that the sheets which the investigators
returned to him were not the same ones which he gave
them on March 3rd.

And there the matter rests. Stale-mate. One can accept
the Air Force's charge that the 66-year-old retired longshoreman was capable of perpetrating an elaborate hoax
—complete with strange footprints, landing gear indentations, a detailed description of an alien, and a convincing
manuscript on peculiar tissue paper—or one can accept
the NICAP's charges that the Air Force is once again
"covering up" a major clue to the UFO mystery.

23.

How Do They Move?

"We are spending millions to develop our own rocket boosters to get our spacecraft to the moon and beyond. Imagine what a great help it would be to get our hands on a ship from another planet and examine its power plant."

Although Major Hector Quintanella might have been only pseudo-serious when he uttered those words, the fact remains that once our scientists discover how the UFO's propel themselves, they will have placed the entire universe at man's disposal.

As early as 1955, after he had completed an extensive study of UFO's for the West German government, Dr. Hermann Oberth, the world's foremost authority on space travel, expressed his conclusion that the UFO's probably originated in another galaxy and that they propelled themselves by distorting the gravitational field. During a press conference in 1959, Dr. Oberth told news media that the United States was trying to duplicate the UFO propulsion system and that soon "man will be able to travel to the moon in craft propelled by electro-magnetic means."

Another exponent of the gravitational distortion or cancellation school of UFO propulsion is the Reverend Guy J. Cyr, S. M. of Lawrence, Massachusetts.

Not long ago, Reverend Cyr wrote: ". . . the search for antigravity ceases to be preposterous, for gravity itself is real. It is often referred to as an attraction between pieces of matter. Symmetrically speaking, there should be a counterpart, named a detraction.

"The writer has good reasons to believe that this detraction is antigravity; that this force, too, is real and objective, with a value of its own, and not just the absence of gravity. He dares go a step further and affirm that this reality is more fundamental than gravity: That it is the impetus given to primordial matter causing the universe to expand, at first as to its subatomic particles and today as to its gigantic units, the galaxies, which generally are hurtling away from us at fantastic speeds.

Reverend Cyr believes that there is a strong possibility that advanced alien cultures have perfected vehicles which use cancellation of the force of gravity as a means of propulsion and that man will eventually learn to do the same.

I think it is safe to assume that if the Air Force had captured a UFO and been able to make heads or tails out of it, they would not be bothering with the same old rocket propulsion methods at Cape Kennedy. By the same token, for those who fear the flying saucers might belong to the Soviet Union, it is logical to assume that since the Russians continue to produce rockets and conventional missiles, they do not have the secrets of UFO propulsion, either.

UFO's do some incredible things by earth science standards. Although a few have been reported with propeller-like appendages or with jet-like exhausts, the typical UFO hovers above the earth with no visible means of support, then shoots away without any apparent build-up, like a bullet shot from a gun. They stop, then start again, slow down to speeds lower than that of conventional aircraft, then accelerate to such speeds that it would seem that any crew would be mashed to pulp.

It is obvious that the Newtonian laws which, combined with Einsteinian concepts, are the basis for much of our scientific world view, either have little bearing on the UFO's or else the extra-terrestrials have learned to surmount certain physical laws—if there truly are any "laws."

It should also be re-emphasized that there are many kinds of UFO's. The "generic" term "flying saucers" has been used in this book, but from the cases cited here, it must be obvious that some are saucer-shaped, some are formed like upside-down ice-cream cones, some are only slightly more elongated than eggs, and so on. Whether the difference in shapes indicates many different models from the same source or denotes the fact that several different cultures are sending expeditions to this planet can be debated at great length by those who have the time for that sort of thing. The point to bear in mind, perhaps, is that as there are many different kinds of saucers there are also, undoubtedly, many different methods of propulsion.

The majority of saucer sightings, for instance, include some sort of electro-magnetic interference such as the stopping of automobile engines, head lights, electric clocks, radios, and so forth. This interference seems to indicate that the power field of the UFO is affecting the performance of electro-magnetically operated vehicles and implements of an earth design. One farmer, who had complained of a saucer that had hovered over his farm for several nights in succession, was left with an incredible jump in his light bill as a strange kind of proof that the UFO had been there and had been interfering with the utilities on his farm.

Several cigar-shaped saucers have been observed with vertical bands running around their middles, and certain scientists have speculated whether or not these bands could be immense solenoid coils, which produce the large magnetic fields associated with the flying saucers. Large "mother ships" with prominent vertical bands have been sighted with smaller UFO's clustered about them, as if the saucers were in the act of "re-charging" or "re-fueling."

Then, of course, we have the saucer sightings where absolutely no electro-magnetic interference was reported. What powered those UFO's?

Take another look at the Newtonian universe, whose three basic laws of motion briefly stated, say:

1) Every body continues in a state of rest or uniform motion along a straight line unless or until it is compelled

to change that state by the action of an exterior force.

2) The rate of change of momentum of a body is proportional to the force acting and takes place in the direction of the straight line in which the force acts.

3) To every action there is an equal and opposite reaction.

Again, we must observe that if the saucers are abiding by our rules and definitions of the physical universe, they are doing impossible things which should have crushed their crews and burned up their spacecraft with atmospheric friction long ago.

Of course, man only names the physical laws, he does not create them. Perhaps earth concepts of what constitutes the physical universe will have to become radically altered to incorporate the new knowledge which other galaxies may someday in the near-future stand ready to impart.

Fantastic as it might seem in 1966, consider the possibility that the UFO's arrive here through teleportation. Teleportation is "the movement of objects, either animate or inanimate, instantaneously, or almost so, from one place to another." In other words, the phenomenon consists of literally passing matter through matter. Space isn't travelled; it is avoided. One does not spend light years traveling through space; one is simply there, instantly, "or almost so."

Charles Fort describes hundreds of cases of unique human beings who possessed the ability to "teleport" themselves or objects from one place to another. Oftentimes, accomplished mediums have affected "teleportation" (or "apport" as spiritualists term the phenomena) during seances. Poltergeist phenomena has been known to produce several dramatic teleportations of fruits, books, pins, clothing, and items of furniture.

If parapsychologists, physical researchers, and physicists are only now beginning to apply serious scientific techniques to the study of teleportation on this planet, isn't it completely feasible that a culture, several million years ahead of ours, has long since learned to employ "mind over matter"? Certainly this theory would require a re-ordering of the universe as it is now known, but has not the "impossible" presence of the saucers already done that?

24.

Aerial Attack Over Elmore, Ohio

Richard Crawford, Chief of Police of Elmore, Ohio, was driving his squad car toward the small town on the night of June 12, 1964 when he did a double-take, noticing a brilliant light off the side of State Route 51. He pulled the car off the side of the road to get a good look at the object. His first thought, that it was an airplane or helicopter, he had immediately rejected, for the object was too bright and had an aura around it that extended for what he estimated to be a quarter of a mile in either direction.

As he watched, Chief Crawford became aware of the deathly silence that hung in the air. The sky overhead was clear, and the stars twinkled their way through the atmosphere to his eyes. Not the slightest wind moved the leaves on the nearby tree. Crawford figured that he would be able to hear the sound of any conventional engine for miles, yet the object which appeared to be less than a mile away made absolutely no sound.

Thinking what he was looking at was perhaps an illuminated blimp, Crawford switched on his spotlight and aimed it at the light in the sky. The object which had been blinking in the sky over Elmore, moved slightly, then began glowing steadily. Wondering whether or not the thing had responded to his light, Chief Crawford blinked the spot twice. Immediately afterward, the object itself blinked twice. Then the scene went black. Crawford watched the area for another five minutes, but the object did not show itself again.

Elmore, a town with a population of 1300, is located about twenty miles southwest of Toledo. Nothing like the bright light and accompanying aura had ever visited the little town before.

Still puzzling over what he had observed in the sky, the Chief continued his nightly duties. He checked the Harris-Elmore School, which is part of his scheduled patrol, at 11:30 P.M. As he was pulling out of the area, the object appeared in the sky again. This time Crawford's view was partially obstructed by trees, but the object itself appeared to be nearer to the ground. The estimated height of his first sighting was about 2,000 feet; this time the Chief guessed it to be at 1,000 feet. Perhaps because it was closer, the object appeared to be considerably larger and brighter than when he had seen it the first time. Once again he shined his spot at the thing, but this time it moved rapidly out of view in a northwesterly direction. Its movement was accompanied by a soft swishing sound, like a fast moving object rushing past one's ear.

Chief Crawford was convinced that there was more to the light than an optical illusion. He switched on his radio and contacted his deputy, Carl Soenichsoen, who was cruising in another squad car. He had considered calling the deputy when he had first sighted the object, but he knew that his voice would have been perfectly audible to anybody with a shortwave radio tuned to the police band. Not wanting to cause a general panic, he told his deputy to meet him in front of a local food market on the outskirts of Elmore.

Soenichsoen was closer to the food market than Crawford had been and beat his chief there by several minutes. When the chief's car pulled up, the deputy got out of his car and ran over to greet him.

"Is that what you're talking about," he asked excitedly, pointing at the bright object. It appeared as it had when Crawford had first seen it. When the deputy had first arrived, the object had been glowing steadily, but by the time Crawford pulled up, it had begun blinking at what the men estimated to be one-second intervals.

Just as before, it was impossible to make out any distinct outline, only a fuzzy ball of light and the large aura that surrounded it. Then, as the two men watched, the object moved from its stationary position, which appeared to be about a mile away over the Ohio turnpike, and headed directly for them. Chief Crawford radioed the state highway patrol while his deputy continued to watch the object. The highway patrol had a plane, and Crawford reasoned that they would be more able to do something about the strange light in the sky than he would. As it approached them, it grew in brightness and size and changed from a nondescript glow to the form of a wedge or V, flying through the sky.

Unable to do anything but watch, the two men looked on as the flying V passed within 500 feet of them. They both clearly described the object later. The top leg of the V was a full third longer than the bottom, and the entire object moved at a "fantastic rate of speed." In a very short time, it had disappeared over the horizon.

Minutes after the thing had vanished, two highway patrolmen arrived on the scene. They were too late to see the strange object, but both Crawford and Soenichsoen related what they had seen.

The state police put in an immediate call to Toledo Express Airport, which is located 10 miles west of Toledo, and, after explaining the sighting, asked for a radar check of the area.

"There is nothing in your area within a radius of 45 miles," came the reply.

The men standing in the parking lot of the food market reasoned that either the object was too low or else it had moved out of the district and the range of the radar. As they discussed the sighting, a propeller-driven plane appeared in the sky. It was easily identifiable as a plane, for its wings and fuselage were properly lighted and the sound of its motor was completely audible. But the plane itself was acting very strangely. It circled dangerously near the ground for night-time flying, yet at no time did it appear to be in any sort of trouble. Furthermore, *it combed the area that the bright object had just vacated.*

Puzzled, the highway patrol officers put in another call to the airport and requested a radar search of the area. The immediate response: "I'm sorry, there's nothing in your area within a radius of 45 miles."

The highway patrolman laughed, explained that four

men had a propeller-driven plane in perfect view, and asked the operator to check again. After a pause, the voice explained that a plane practicing night landings had wandered over Elmore. The radar operator suggested that perhaps that was what Crawford and Soenichsoen had seen.

The suggestion was not convincing to the two men who had watched the antics of a strange object passing over the Ohio skies. Too many things were not accounted for by that explanation. The sound of the motor driven plane was heard only after the light had vanished from view. Furthermore, such conventional craft do not have the ability to hover in one spot, or to carry an aura of light along for the ride, or to change shape at will.

Chief Crawford is certain that what he saw was no conventional type aircraft. The lack of any sound to distinguish it as a jet or a prop-type aircraft, and its ability to hover and then to move at speeds too great to be duplicated by any known variety of airplane has led him to suspect that it was ". . . either a highly sophisicated military craft . . . or a craft from outer space."

He is inclined to believe that Elmore was visited by a vehicle from outer space, and he thinks, for good reason. Elmore is the location of a plant which produces beryllium. The metal is light, durable, and has a high melting point. It is useful in many alloys with copper and aluminum and is an integral element in atomic age construction. If an alien power wanted an index of a civilization's advancement in technical areas, a good standard would be the rate of production of beryllium.

The metal itself is so light that dust and shavings, which occur during processing, carry easily on any air current. Concentration of beryllium in an air sample could be used to determine how much of the metal is in production.

Chief Crawford points out that this is simply a theory, but he wonders why else such strange objects would be in the sky over the little town of Elmore.

25.

UFO's in the Deep Freeze

"Revealed! The Underground world of supermen discovered by Admiral Byrd under the North Pole . . . and kept secret by U.S. Government. Dr. Raymond Bernard . . . New York University, noted scholar and author of *The Hollow Earth,* says that the true home of the flying saucers is a huge underground world whose entrance is at the North Polar opening. In the hollow interior of the Earth lives a super race which wants nothing to do with man on the surface. They launched their flying saucers only after man threatened the world with A-Bombs.

"Admiral Byrd, according to sources quoted by Dr. Bernard, led a Navy team into the polar opening and came upon this underground region. It is free of ice and snow, has mountains covered with forests; lakes, rivers and strange animals. But the news of his discovery was suppressed by the U.S. Government in order to prevent other nations from exploring the inner world and claiming it." (From an advertisement for *The Hollow Earth,* Fieldcrest Publishing Company.)

Although the forbidden knowledge claimed to be revealed by Dr. Bernard's book might stretch the bounds of credulity possessed by most people, after last summer's flurry of UFO activity in the polar regions—especially Antarctica—military personnel stationed in the earth's "deepfreeze" are almost willing to accept even such a tale of an "underground world of supermen" to account for the phenomena which they observed.

The value of sightings that occur in the Antarctic lies in the fact that the only people there to make the observations are trained scientific personnel. Not only have the scientific outposts seen the objects, but they have attempted to photograph them. The secretary of the Argentine navy made the following statement to the press, which was reprinted in Buenos Aires newspapers.

"The Navy garrison in the Argentine Antarctica (Deception Island) observed, on July 3, at 19:40 hours (local time) a giant lens-shaped flying object, solid in appearance, color mostly red and green, changing occasionally, with yellow, blue, white, and orange shades. The object was moving on a zigzagging trajectory toward the east but several times it changed course to the west and north with varied speeds and no sound. It passed at an elevation of 45 degrees over the horizon, distance estimated at about 10 to 15 kilometers from the base.

"During the maneuvers performed by the object the witnesses were able to register its tremendous speeds and also the fact that it hovered motionless for about 15 minutes at an estimated altitude of about 5,000 meters (3.10 miles). The meteorological conditions for the area of the sighting can be considered as very good for this time of the year: clear sky, some strato-cumulus, moon in the last quarter and perfect visibility.

"The object was witnessed by the meteorologist together with 13 members of the garrison and three Chilean sub-officers visiting the base. The observation lasted for 20 minutes and photographs of the object were taken.

"On the afternoon of the same day the same object was observed from the Argentine base on the South Orkney Islands, moving away toward the northwest, elevation 30 degrees over the horizon, distance estimated at about 10 to 15 kilometers (six to nine miles). The Chilean base also observed the object referred to above the afternoon of that same day."

The Argentine bases in the Antarctic are some of the oldest of the southern scientific outposts. Each is equipped with sensitive equipment for detecting changes in the magnetic field of the area. On July 3, 1965, all of this equipment was functioning properly, and they all registered abnormal changes in the magnetic field around the bases.

A later press release made by the secretary of the Argentine navy gave a more detailed account of the sighting, which only confirmed the object's mysterious nature. The commander of the Argentine base at Deception Island said that all seventeen men under his command had seen the object, including three Chilean sub officers, who were visiting the base because one of them had a broken arm that needed medical attention.

An interesting passage in the report states, ". . . information from the Navy garrison at South Orkney Islands calls attention to a fact of extreme importance; during the passage of the strange object over that base, two variometers working in perfect condition registered disturbances in the magnetic field which were recorded on their tapes."

This release also explained that the probability that the photos would yield conclusive results were low, since the area was dark and the film used was of low sensitivity. It was impossible for the film to be immediately processed, as the bases were unreached in the middle of the Antarctic winter when they were taken.

On the same day, July 7, 1965, the Ministry of Defense in Santiago, Chile released the contents of their sightings to the press. The first observation occurred on June 18th and was reported by Commander Mario Jahn Barrera.

"I have to report that today at 4:00 P.M. (local time) was sighted from this base an aerial object, luminous intensity of a first magnitude star, appearing east of the island at 60 degrees elevation, changing direction to the left in a 180-degree turn to the west and then turning 90 degrees to the right; moving away to the south following an irregular trajectory at 4:20 P.M. Meteorological conditions good, dark sky. The phenomenon was observed by all in the garrison."

A report on the object which the Argentine base had sighted on July 3rd was also released.

"Sergeant Moya, in the course of meteorological observations on July 3, spotted the presence of an aerial object sighted for 20 minutes by nine members of the garrison. Red-yellow luminosity, changing colors, elevation 45 degrees, crossing the island at SW in a NW-SE direction. High velocity, oscillatory course, luminosity first magnitude star. Good conditions of visibility. Communications on the same day, at 20:30 hours (local time), with the English base revealed that on July 2, at 19:45 hours, five members of that garrison had sighted celestial object north of the island, moving in a zigzagging course, stopping in mid-air for five or ten minutes and disappearing in a vertical direction. Red-yellow color changing to green, elevation 20 degrees and brightness first magnitude star.

"Communication with the Argentine Base, Deception Island, disclosed that, on July 3, 16 persons including three Chilean sub officers had observed an aerial object over the northern area of the island moving in a north-northeast direction, varying speed, oscillatory course, changing yellow-green-orange color, leaving a contrail at 30 degrees elevation. Round-shaped, disappearing into cirrus clouds. Was tracked by theodolites and high-powered binoculars. Corporal Duran, from this garrison, took 10 color photographs through the theodolite. Still on the same day, at the Argentine base at Orkney Island, two meteorological observers sighted an aerial object flying at high speed on a parabolic trajectory, course E-W, white luminosity, causing disturbance in the magnetic field registered on geomagnetic instruments with patterns notably out of the normal.

"There was no previous communication between the bases listed above that could produce a psychosis of this kind of observation—which must be of great interest for scientific organizations interested."

The release of these two communiques by the Chilean Defense Ministry sent reporters scurrying to their typewriters, but soon they were back knocking at the door, hungry for more. An interview, via radio, was granted with the commanding officer of the Chilean base, Mario Jahn Barrera. The radio was handled by Commander

Jose Berichevski, Chief of Public Relations for the Chilean Air Force, from the Air Force radio-operations center in Santiago.

Barrera minced no words, "It is nonsense to say that we saw a flying saucer like those from science fiction stories. What we sighted was something real, a solid object which was moving at incredible speeds, performed maneuvers, emitted a greenish light, and caused interference in the electro-magnetic instruments of the Argentine base situated close to ours, on a small island.

"Its red-yellow color changed to green and orange. It was flying at a short distance from the base at an elevation of 45 degrees, over the north of the island, and moving in a zigzagging course.

"It hovered in mid-air after performing one of its maneuvers, remaining motionless for about 20 minutes and then moving away at high speed. We observed this object through high-powered binoculars.

"I don't believe it could be an airship of terrestrial manufacture. As an officer in the Chilean Air Force, my knowledge about man-made machines gives me absolute conviction that nothing similar exists on the earth: in shape, velocity and mobility in space. We have taken 10 color photographs which will be developed in Santiago.

"As soon as we sighted the object we tried to contact by radio the Argentine and English bases. But such contact was impossible because there was a very strong interference on the radio, on all channels. With the radio useless and under intense emotion we continued to observe the thing in space, on a clear night without winds . . ."

26.

Space Ship on a Minnesota Highway

A 19-year-old radio announcer for station KEYL of Long Prairie, Minnesota, James Townsend, was moving west along Highway 27 about four miles east of Long Prairie on October 23, 1965. The time was approximately 7:15 P.M. and, as the young man rounded a curve at a good rate of speed, he was confronted by a tall, standing object in the middle of the road.

Slamming on the brakes, the announcer's 1956 model car skidded to a halt, 20 feet in front of what he described as a rocket ship. Immediately, the motor, lights, and radio of his car stopped functioning, although the scene in front of him remained illuminated. The rocket ship was shaped like a cylinder with a blunt taper on one end, and, although it was only about ten feet in diameter, Townsend estimated that it was over 30 feet in height. Realizing the consequences of such a find, the announcer's immediate thought was to knock the thing over and retain the ultimate evidence of his sighting. But the car would not turn over when he twisted the key in the ignition.

The tall, narrow craft looked to be unstable, sitting on its protruding fins in the middle of the highway. Townsend thought that he might be able to tip the craft by hand. Jumping out of the car, he began an advance for the apparently deserted rocket.

But the young announcer was astonished when three incredible looking objects moved out to meet him. These things were in the shape of small cylinders and moved on spindly looking legs, which were no thicker than pencils. Although they had no distinguishing features, Townsend

126

described their movements to be more like creatures than robots.

Townsend had no idea how long he and the objects confronted each other, but he said it "seemed like forever." Then he retreated to his car, and the little can-like beings moved back toward their rocket. They disappeared in the brilliant beam of light that glared under the main section of the rocket. Then, as the radio announcer watched out the windshield of his car, the light became even more intense, and a humming sound crescendoed in volume until it hurt Townsend's ear drums. As the rocket lifted off, it reminded the radio announcer of a glowing flashlight, and the scene east of Long Prairie, Minnesota was lit "as bright as day." Once the thing was airborne, the light in the bottom went out.

As Townsend watched the vehicle ascend into the sky, the lights and the radio of his car came on. The car which he had been unable to start only minutes before *began running by itself*. Townsend later said he was sure he had not touched the starter, even though the car had been left in park, and the ignition remained on.

Unnerved, Townsend turned his car around and sped back to Long Prairie. Without hesitation he went directly to the sheriff's office to report what he had seen. With considerable effort, Sheriff James Bain and police officer Luvern Lubitz were able to calm the excited young man. Both of these men later confirmed that Townsend had obviously been badly frightened. Sheriff Bain described him as "excited, nervous, and shaky," while Lubitz observed that he was "not his natural color."

The first thing Townsend said to these men was: "I am not crazy nor am I drunk; neither am I ignorant."

Sheriff Bain and Lubitz agreed with the statement, although they did not know why Townsend had said it at first. All who know James Townsend later testified that he is a level-headed, hard-working young man, not known to drink. Furthermore, he has strong religious convictions and had spent the summer as a counselor at a Bible camp.

Both men at the sheriff's office listened to his story and

acted immediately. Although Townsend was reluctant to go, Sheriff Bain and Lubitz convinced him that he should take them to the spot where he had seen the strange craft.

After driving out to the spot, all three of the men simultaneously observed a peculiar orange light moving in the northern sky. Lubitz thought it was "more yellow white than orange, flickering off and on and leaving a sort of yellow tail."

A close inspection of the spot where the rocket ship had been standing showed that three strips of an oil-like substance had been left on the pavement. They were three feet long and four inches wide, running parallel to the highway. Lubitz said that he had never seen anything like those marks, left on any kind of surface. After puzzling over it for some time, the men returned to Long Prairie. Sheriff Bain was unable to determine any reason for the marks that had been left on the pavement other than the fantastic tale that Townsend had told him.

It did not take long before the story was sizzling over the country via the wire services. Instant reactions to Townsend's story varied from praise of his courage, to ridicule of his "fantastic imagination." Many of the residents of Minnesota had been left with an open mind after a late summer and fall of heavily concentrated UFO activity. On August 2nd, UFO sightings had been reported all over the Midwest, and nearly every one of the police on duty in Minneapolis in the early hours of the morning had seen strange lights in the sky.

Although the story was given favorable and fair treatment by some of the news media, others either openly ridiculed the tale or gave explicit indications of their private prejudices on the matter. Townsend received all sorts of crank mail, and people traveled for miles just to have the opportunity of calling him a liar or a drunk.

One newspaper account claimed that Townsend had been studying an article on UFO's in a current issue of a national magazine and implied that the rocket and the cylinder men were manifestations of the radio announcer's imagination. After one week of such distasteful business,

Townsend refused any more interviews. "I'm sorry I ever reported the incident," he said.

But more than a few people took what Townsend had said seriously. UFO investigators from all over the country tried to contact him. WCCO television of Minneapolis gave him the opportunity to explain the story himself. The *Late Don Dahl Show* provided a receptive atmosphere in which Townsend could relate his story without fearing that the interviewer would resort to mockery and innuendo over the open microphone.

With such widespread publicity, corroborating accounts turned up. Ray Blessing, the 14-year-old son of Mr. Frank Blessing, a Minneapolis businessman, was operating his three-inch 200-power reflector telescope when he saw a "Buck Rogers-like thing" pass in front of his lens for exactly fifteen minutes (7:00 P.M. October 23rd) before James Townsend had slammed on his brakes to avoid hitting the standing rocket. Blessing described an inverted sombrero which he had been able to study carefully as it passed across the sky from horizon to horizon. Although the young astronomer reported the sighting to his parents at the time, they did nothing until they heard Townsend tell his story on television.

Back in Long Prairie, three boys who were out hunting raccoon claimed that they had seen a strange light in the sky, about the same time that Townsend had come across the rocket in the middle of Highway 27. Other residents of the area reported to Police Officer Lubitz that they had seen strange things around the little community, but did not want their names to be made public.

To summarize: James Townsend slammed on his brakes in order to avoid hitting a tall rocket ship. He saw three cylindrical figures, and he saw the rocket take off and disappear. When Sheriff Bain, Lubitz, and he returned to the scene, they saw a peculiar "orange light" in the northern sky. Numerous other sightings were reported at the time, and three mysterious strips had been left on the pavement. It is easy to understand why James Townsend is convinced that what he saw was real.

27.

Don't Blame Con-Edison

Robert Walsh, deputy city aviation commissioner of Syracuse, New York was flying a private plane over the city when the lights went out. It was 5:22 P.M. on November 9, 1965—a day which shall long be remembered by residents of the Eastern Seaboard as the Big Blackout.

Walsh managed to effect a safe landing, and once on the ground, worked to bring other aircraft down safely.

While he was sitting on the ground with several other men, "a strange thing happened . . . we saw a sudden ball of fire south of us—toward Thompson Road and Carrier traffic circle.

"It appeared to be about 100 feet in the air and 50 feet in diameter. All I could think of was a mushroom effect."

Ten minutes later, the group of men saw another ball of fire, similar to the first.

"I have yet to see an explanation," Walsh told a reporter for the Syracuse *Herald-Journal*.

Was the Big Blackout, which put 80,000 square miles and several of America's largest cities "in the dark," caused by UFO originated electro-magnetic interference? Many people seem to think so and back up their allegation with eye-witness sightings of glowing saucers in the area only minutes before the lights went out, plunging 30,000,000 persons into total darkness in seven U.S. states and parts of Canada.

Weldon Ross of Syracuse was preparing to land his private airplane at Hancock field when he saw a UFO "about 100 feet in diameter" near the New York Power Company. As he watched, the object next passed over the

New York Central Railroad tracks between Lake Oneida and Hancock Field.

Did the electro-magnetic field of the UFO trigger the progressive overloads as it passed over the New York Power Company plant near Hancock Airport?

Ross, a flight instructor who was with a student, James Brooking, said that "a ball of orange-reddish fire which flared up bigger than a house fire" hovered over the high line, which runs from Clay to Niagara Falls, for about 10 seconds.

Mr. and Mrs. John Derr of Somerville, New Jersey reported seeing "a very large light, larger than the evening star" moving to the Northeast moments after their lights had gone out.

Tom Doxsee of Manlius, near Syracuse, also reported seeing a ball of fire "some time within an hour of the time the lights went out."

The NICAP has collected more than 100 cases of local blackouts allegedly caused by electro-magnetic effects of UFO's. Admittedly, none have been as dramatic as the Eastern Seaboard blackout, and most have concerned themselves with small power plants and automobile headlights. Some, however, were ambitious enough to seem to be leading up to a grand *coup*.

On September 25, 1965, the tropical resort town of Cuernavaca, Mexico suffered three consecutive power blackouts in less than an hour. Electric company officials were baffled and completely unable to account for the puzzling failures. Several residents, tourists, police officers, airport officials, and control tower operators at the International Airport had spotted UFO's over the area at the time of the blackouts. Authorities could not help drawing a parallel between the arrival of the flying saucers and the retreat of electrical power.

Also in September of 1965, a UFO practically skimmed the rooftops in Mexico City as it dropped down to an estimated 30 feet. Witnesses could clearly note that it was about 25 feet in diameter with a row of glowing portholes. So many autmobiles were stopped by electro-magnetic interference from the object that traffic practically came to a standstill.

About a month after the dramatic blackout on the Eastern Seaboard, on December 2nd, another large-area power failure blacked out four important military bases and turned the lights out on a million inhabitants in New Mexico, Texas, and Mexico.

President Lyndon B. Johnson ordered a federal investigation into the reasons why crucial military bases should have been plunged into the dark, endangering national security. On that same day, several counties in Pennsylvania complained of dimming lights and local blackouts. Again, the sky was full of UFO's.

One does not have to have a great fund of imagination to appreciate implications of flying saucers blacking out military bases. If the UFO's truly have the ability to scramble power plants, National Defense becomes a bad joke.

If, as many believe, the saucers were responsible for the power failures, was the Big Blackout a test of power or simply a way of saying, "Hello, down there; start taking us seriously?"

Don't blame Con-Edison. They may have been scapegoats for a cosmic caper.

28.

Strange Visitors in Exeter, New Hampshire

Shortly after midnight on September 3, 1965, Officer Eugene Bertrand of the Exeter, New Hampshire police force pulled up beside a parked automobile on Route 101 near Exeter.

The automobile was occupied by two nervous women, who, in between near hysterical gasps, told Officer Bertrand that they had been pursued by a bright red, flashing, airborne object that had followed them for nearly 12 miles. They had to calm down a bit before they dared to drive on. Their nerves had been shattered by the harrowing ordeal.

Officer Bertrand shook his head with a wry smile as he drove away from the frightened ladies. His perceptive nose had told him that the ladies had not been drinking, but they had obviously frightened themselves into believing that some weird, glowing object had chased them. Probably just the reflection of the moon off a fender. With the newspapers carrying all those stories about people seeing flying saucers, it was no wonder that two ladies driving alone at night had convinced themselves that they were being followed by something unearthly.

The policeman made a routine report of the alleged sighting and settled back in the cushions for a long night of driving on patrol. At least the two ladies had given him something to chuckle about. It got lonely just driving around Exeter.

But the events of September 3rd would not allow Officer Bertrand to be lonely on that particular evening.

At about 2:30 A.M., Bertrand received a call from Patrolman Reginald Toland, who was on duty at the desk, asking him to report to the stationhouse. When Bertrand arrived, he was met by Toland and a very shaken Norman Muscarello, 18, of Exeter, who had been hitchhiking home from Amesbury, Massachusetts. According to Muscarello, a huge glowing ball had come out of the sky directly at him. He had flung himself into a ditch and had taken refuge beside a stone wall. The UFO, which he estimated to be about 80 feet in diameter, had bright red flashing lights and seemed to be a solid aircraft of unconventional design.

Officer Bertrand interrupted the teen-ager long enough to briefly report his earlier experience with the two women, who had described essentially the same object.

Norman Muscarello went on to tell the policemen how the silently hovering craft had moved on to rest above a nearby farmhouse, illuminating the entire area. At last, it had moved on far enough to encourage the young man to leave his sheltering wall and make a run for the farmhouse.

He banged on the door, roused the farmer, but the man could not make any sense of the excited words that the frightened Norman Muscarello was babbling. Norman staggered away from the farmhouse, ran back onto the highway where he had been picked up by a middle-aged couple who brought him to the police station.

When he ran into the stationhouse, Officer Toland had immediately seen that the boy was near shock. He gave Muscarello a cigarette, forced him to calm down a bit before he began an incredible rush of words about some mysterious flying object. When Toland had sorted out Muscarello's story and made sense of it, he put in the call for fellow-officer Bertrand.

Bertrand remained frankly skeptical. It was obvious that Muscarello and the two ladies had seen something, but they simply had to be mistaking some kind of natural phenomenon for this monstrous glowing ball that had allegedly pursued each of them.

The officers decided that Muscarello should take Officer Bertrand to the spot where he had seen the UFO. At first the teen-ager warmed to the idea like a man who has been asked to volunteer for suicide mission, but at last, he consented to accompany Bertrand to the field between the two farmhouses where he had squatted beside the stone wall.

Bertrand spent most of the time it took to drive out to the area in attempt to calm Muscarello. The youth was still shaken from his former experience with the object and did not relish a second confrontation. When they arrived in the area, Officer Bertrand parked his cruiser beside the highway, and told Toland that he and the teen-ager were going to leave the car and walk out into a field.

It was a clear night, moonless and warm. The two men had walked about 100 yards out onto the field, when Muscarello shouted: "There it is!"

"He was right," Bertrand said later. "It was coming up over a row of trees. There was no noise at all. It was about 100 feet away in the air, and about 200 feet away from us. I could see five bright red lights in a straight row. They dimmed from right to left and then from left to right—just as an advertising sign does. . . ."

Livestock in the fields and in pens next to the barn began to stamp and make nervous sounds of fear. Dogs near the farmhouses began to howl. Bertrand noticed that the entire area was bathed in a blood-red light, and, fearing infra-red rays, he grabbed the teen-ager and they ran for the shelter of the patrol car. Calling Officer Toland back at the station, he shouted: "My God! I see the damn thing myself!"

After listening to a few minutes of an incredible conversation between officers Toland and Bertrand, Officer Dave Hunt arrived at the field in another cruiser.

Hunt was able to see the object "going from left to right, between the tops of two big trees" and was able to clearly distinguish the "pulsating lights."

The UFO had no sooner moved out of the sight of the officers and the frightened Muscarello boy when Toland received a call from the Exeter night operator. The operator reported a man "so hysterical he could hardly talk straight" who had called from a pay phone to tell her that a flying saucer was heading straight for him. The call had been disconnected while the man was still screaming excitedly into the mouthpiece.

The next morning, Lieutenant Cottrell of the Exeter Police listened patiently to the story his three officers told him. "If I didn't believe these guys," he said later, "I'd put 'em in a locked room and give 'em some blocks to play with."

The Manchester *Union-Leader* and the Exeter *News-Letter* gave full coverage to the incident and listed several other reports of sightings by citizens of irreproachable reputation. Only the unconvincible, professional skeptics of the Air Force remained to classify the sightings in the officially approved categories of "airplane lights" or "St. Elmo's fire."

John G. Fuller, intrigued by the fact that the Oklahoma State Police had released a nine-page report contradicting Air Force analysis of sightings made by members of the police force in their state during the busy saucer summer of 1965, devoted his October 2nd "Trade Winds" column in the *Saturday Review* to the incessant contradictions between information given by saucer sighters and the subsequent evaluation of the reports by the Air Force. Deciding to apply in-depth reportage to the sightings at Exeter, Fuller traveled up to the New Hampshire town and tape-recorded interviews with over 60 people who had seen UFO's.

In an article entitled "Outer-Space Ghost Story" in the February 22, 1966 issue of *Look,* Fuller dealt with some of the sightings that he had discussed with the citizens of the Exeter area. He learned, for example, that: "Near Bessie's Lunch, in Fremont, dozens of cars would gather nightly at the base of the power lines, along which the objects would hover.

"The Jalbert family living beside the power lines, reported constant sightings, dull-orange discs moving erratically along the lines.

"The Chief of Police of Fremont, along with a half-dozen members of his family, saw an object hovering over his house and barn. An outside light, operated by a photo-electric cell, went out when the object appeared."

The folks around Exeter, New Hampshire do not pay much attention to Air Force disclaimers anymore. They know that something strange visited their village last September.

29.

Swamp Gas or Spacecraft in Michigan?

Frank Mannor, 47, who rents a farmhouse outside of Dexter, Michigan, and his 19-year-old son, Ronald, were astonished when a triangular-shaped object with flashing red and green lights dipped near them and then hovered over a swamp 500 yards from them. The Mannors were among a score of people who described similar objects in the Michigan skies of March 21, 1966.

The Associated Press carried an account in which Mannor described what he saw. "It was almost flat on the bottom, and kind of high and peaked on top. We couldn't see much except the outline and the lights at the ends, because the whole thing was wrapped in a light like a halo, and it kept shimmering.

"It was like watching something across the desert. You know how the heat waves keep changing what you see."

Mannor and his son investigated the swamp after the object had disappeared. "We went down into the swamp, but there was nothing. No smell of an exhaust."

Douglas J. Harvey, Sheriff of Washtenaw County in which Dexter is located, at first was openly skeptical of the validity of the sightings. "I didn't believe these reports," said Harvey in an AP interview. "But with so many trained police personnel and reliable citizens having seen them, I must believe something is in the Washtenaw County skies."

The sighting of a Dexter patrolman, Robert Huniwell, may well have killed the sheriff's skepticism. The police officer reported an object with red and green flashing lights which, at one time, hovered "within ten feet" of the patrol car.

Weston Vivian, a Democratic Congressman from Michigan, conferred with Sheriff Harvey and other citizens of the area and planned to ask the Defense Department to investigate the strange sightings after similar objects had been reported in the skies over Michigan three times within the week.

As usual, official reactions were skeptical. Dr. Allen J. Hynek, an astrophysicist from Northwestern University and special consultant for the U.S. Air Force, dismissed the Michigan sightings as "swamp gas."

Sightings of the strange lights came from other areas besides Michigan. R. D. Landversicht, an Ohio Highway patrolman, reported seeing strange lights approaching Wright-Patterson Air Force Base near Dayton. An amateur photographer, Landversicht photographed the object and turned the film over to Air Force officials at Wright-Patterson.

But this was not the first attempt at photographing the strange lights. In Michigan, another unidentified photographer tried his luck at recording the flying objects on film. Hynek, the astrophysicist from Northwestern, said that the photographs, "without any question" were time exposures of the rising moon and the planet Venus.

In a letter to the editors of the Cedar Rapids, Iowa *Gazette,* Robert Lynn, of the same city and associate Member of NICAP, pointed out that Hynek's statement about the photograph was untenable.

"Help!" Lynn began. "Someone get Dr. Hynek, astrophysicist and Air Force scientific consultant, an almanac. In Friday and Saturday night's paper, he states that the photograph taken in or near Ann Arbor on the 16th (or 17th—both dates were given for the same photograph) is "without any question," a time exposure of the rising moon and the planet Venus. The photograph was taken at 3:30 A.M.

"One source says that on the 16th the moon rose at 3:37 A.M. Another source gives an additional two minute margin for these days. In either case, the photo was taken BEFORE the moon rose.

"Let's say that the photo was taken on the 16th (moon

rose at 3:37 A.M.) Considering the length of the trail of the 'ten minute' exposure, the object had been over the horizon for approximately 40 minutes (assuming that the object maintained a uniform speed).

"The difference between the time the picture was taken, and the time the moon rose is approximately seven minutes. This seven minutes, plus the 40 minutes since it had risen, equals 47 minutes. Therefore, the photo was taken 47 minutes BEFORE the moon was in that position. On the 17th, the difference would be about 88 minutes.

"This mistake is comparable to his assumption that the unidentified flying object (with red and green flashing lights), sighted in Michigan, were the result of the release of 'swamp gas.' "

Shortly after the sightings in Michigan, lights were reported over Wisconsin and Ohio as well. A member of Toledo's Sylvania fire department observed some of the objects with binoculars. In a report to a local radio station, the man described four objects which ranged in color from red to green to white. "They kind of look like a star when you first see them, but they blink on and off," was his description.

Near Dayton, Ohio at Wright-Patterson Air Force Base, Project Blue Book chief Major Hector Quintanella, in an official statement, said, "It's not unusual after incidents such as these in Michigan last week to get a lot of 'sighting' reports. It's a normal aftermath pattern."

But such comments are little comfort to those people who walk outside of their houses and see objects that "officially" do not exist. Not everyone is convinced that such sightings can be passed off so easily. Gerald R. Ford, Republican representative from Michigan, thinks that the situation merits a national investigation. He feels that the incidents in Michigan are "sufficient to justify some action by our government."

On the radio-television program, *Face the Nation,* Representative Ford said: "Bring out these witnesses from the Air Force and the National Aeronautics and Space Administration, have them interrogated by members of the House or Senate committee, let them put their records on the line. Let the people who have allegedly seen these objects come and testify."

Ford had hardly made his proposal when a new sighting was made in the Ann Arbor-Dexter area, this one by an aeronautical engineer who said: "I have a distinct feeling that this was an electronics phenomenon."

Emile Grenier, 55, said that he watched "a brilliant light in the sky" for about two minutes as it performed what he described as "an impossible maneuver" before it ostensibly settled into a grove of trees just outside of Ann Arbor.

"The light was traveling at 150 to 200 miles an hour," said Grenier, who lives nearby, "then came to an instant stop."

Lawrence Espey, a University of Michigan physiologist, said that he had seen essentially the same thing as he was driving in the area.

Grenier told newsmen: "I know of nothing that could cancel mass (i.e. to make an object virtually weightless, giving it full maneuverability) as this thing obviously did from the speed of a small airplane to zero instantly."

The area in which Grenier and Espey reported their sightings is less than a quarter mile from the University of Michigan's nuclear research space laboratory. Dr. Hynek had confined his investigation to sightings made near Dexter and at Hillsdale. Dexter is about 50 miles southwest of Detroit, Hillsdale about 100 miles west.

Dexter Police Chief Taylor expressed his doubts over the astrophysicist's analysis of the "pyramid-shaped object" that the Mannor family and several of his patrolmen had seen. "I have no idea what it was, but I don't think it was swamp gas. There's something else to it."

Hillsdale County Civil Defense Director William Van Horn was openly dissatisfied with Dr. Hynek's explanation. Van Horn and 87 Hillsdale College coeds had spent nealy three hours watching a red and white object, about 20 feet in diameter, from dormitory windows.

"I think I will disprove Hynek in a few weeks," Van Horn said.

The Lansing, Michigan *State Journal* observed that "two years ago an investigator checking saucer reports predicted Michigan would have more saucer reports as work at the university progressed."

Shortly after the Air Force's analysis, which attributed the Michigan incidents to "marsh gas," Donald E. Keyhoe, head of NICAP, repeated his charges to newsmen that the Pentagon has a top level policy of discounting all UFO reports.

On Wednesday, March 30th, a spokesman for the Air Force called a press conference to state that the Pentagon had "an open mind about UFO's" and "made no attempt to hush talk about flying saucers."

Pooh-poohing allegations that the Air Force tried to squelch saucer sightings, the spokesman continued: "In the first place, we'd be utterly foolish to try to keep people from telling about something they've seen with their own eyes. Our job is to explain what is seen—not necessarily to change anybody's mind."

That same week, Roscoe Drummond, in his nationally syndicated column, re-echoed House Republican Leader Ford's suggestion that a "Warren Commission-type panel . . . seems to be in order."

Drummond called for a "more credible and detached appraisal of the evidence than we are now getting" from what the columnist termed the "expert unbelievers."

The Washington columnist expressed the frustration of an entire nation when he wrote: "You can't dismiss the possibility that some of the unidentified flying objects . . . which so many people have sighted in so many different places—are real, not imaginary.

"There are, of course UFO buffs who seem to want to believe everything and discount all kinds of logical explanations.

"But Air Force officials assigned to check up on these sightings seem so bored and totally skeptical that many here have the impression that they think the public would go panicky if all the facts were brought into the open.

"The time has come for either the President or Congress to name an objective and respected panel to investigate, appraise and report on all present and future evidence about what is going on.

"We need to get all the data drawn together in one place and examined far more objectively than anyone has done so far. A stable public opinion will come from a trustworthy look at the evidence, not from belittling it."

It would seem that, at the rate reports of phenomena continue to flow into official departments, it is indeed time for "an objective and respected panel to investigate, appraise and report" on UFO sightings in a manner that seems more cognizant of the rights and intelligence of free people, who are entitled to know the truth about matters of national security and who deserve to be treated with respect and dignity when they summon the courage to report unnatural phenomena.

"People are trying to make a fanatic out of me," Frank Mannor of Dexter Township, Michigan complained to *Life's* Paul O'Neil. "They was tramping around here at 3 o'clock this morning and look at them now. They say, 'How much money are you going to make off this?' That's crazy. I don't want no money. I didn't want no publicity in the first place. I don't want none now. I'm just a simple fellow. But I seen what I seen and nobody's going to tell me different. That wasn't no old foxfire or hulla-billusion. It was an object. Maybe it'll come back if all these people would stay away and we could get a picture and have verification of it. Anybody wants to give me a lie-detector test I'll take it."

30.

The Air Force and the UFO

In the January 1965 issue of *True* magazine, Donald E. Keyhoe, director of the National Investigations Committee on Aerial Phenomena (NICAP) charged the U.S. Air Force with deliberately censoring information concerning flying saucers.

Since the early 1950's, Keyhoe has been regularly repeating his charges that, while the Air Force has been seriously analyzing UFO data in secret, it has maintained a policy of officially debunking saucer stories for the press and ridiculing all citizens who report sightings.

"Now the tactic has changed," according to Keyhoe's article. "The tactic is total suppression of news. By a strict Air Force order, entitled AF 200-2, Air Force personnel are forbidden to talk in public about UFO sightings, and information about UFO's is to be withheld from the press unless the thing seen 'has been positively identified as a familiar or known object.'"

Although Keyhoe acknowledges that indirect pressure can be exerted on employees of companies working on defense projects and other areas subject to government control, the retired Marine Corps major has never allowed himself to be restrained by any Air Force edict. In the *True* article, Keyhoe accuses the Air Force of censoring several items which the public has deserved to know. Among them: Four "spacecraft of unknown origin" cruised up to the two-man *Gemini* space capsule on April 8, 1964 when it was on its first orbit, inspected it, then blasted off; on January 10, 1961, a UFO flew so close to a *Polaris* missile that it botched up the radar for 14 minutes; a possible "recharging" operation of UFO's near Canberra, Australia on May 15, 1964.

On March 28, 1966, after the saucer "flap" in Michigan, Keyhoe was once again repeating his charges that "the Pentagon has a top level policy of discounting all UFO reports and over the past several years has used ridicule to discredit sightings."

On Wednesday, March 30th, spokesmen for the Air Force called a press conference to insist that they kept an open mind about UFO's and to deny any "hushing" of saucer reports. In the case of the recent Michigan sightings, a spokesman said, "marsh gas was pin-pointed as the source of colored lights observed by a number of people."

At about the same time as the Air Force press conference, three space scientists called their own press meeting at a convention in Baltimore, Maryland.

Dr. Paul A. Campbell, a pioneer in space medicine, expressed his belief that UFO's are "all in the minds of those who report seeing them."

Dr. John S. Hall, an astronomer at Lowell Observatory in Arizona, felt that tourists from outer space would "certainly have more sophisticated tastes than the sightings indicate."

"I'm concerned about those who see flying saucers," said Dr. Edward C. Walsh. "So many airline pilots report seeing them. That's why I take the train."

Dr. Campbell called the UFO's a "mechanism for escaping from more earthly troubles and worries. People are anxious to believe that there is intelligent life on other planets. They see flying saucers because they want to see them."

Astronomer Hall became a bit whimsical when he wondered, for the benefit of the assembled newsmen, why a civilization with technology so advanced that it could send a manned and maneuverable space ship a distance of at least three light years, would have that spaceship hover over swamps in Michigan or cross-roads in Oklahoma. "They could be peek-a-booing Paris, New York, or London!"

The Air Force has a special public relations office which answers thousands of letters a year from people who want to know more about UFO's. School children, corporate officials, housewives, flying saucer club members, and foreign citizens are only a few of the representative groups of the inquisitive. Last year it sent out 3,717 replies to queries about UFO's. The count for January and February, 1966 had already exceeded 800 requests for information or explanations, even before the deluge that poured in after the recent Michigan sightings.

Some Air Force replies practically constitute a form letter which says that the Air Force has no pictures of flying saucers, that it does not censor or keep secret reports about flying saucers, and that Congress has not yet seen fit to conduct an investigation into the matter of UFO's.

Nearly all requests for materials are accompanied by an annual report of Project Blue Book.

"I've looked at the records of nearly every UFO case back to 1947," Major Hector Quintanella, Jr., a physicist who heads Project Bluebook, said recently. "And my feeling is that the vast majority have involved simple misinterpretation of natural phenomena."

Project Blue Book, started in 1947, has produced what the Air Force considers a satisfactory explanation for 9,501 of a total of 10,147 sightings reported through 1965. Of the 646 unexplained UFO incidents, the official statement is: "The description of the object or its motion cannot be correlated with any known object or phenomenon."

The staff of Project Blue Book is assigned to carry out three main functions: 1) to try to find an explanation for all reported sightings of UFO's, 2) to determine whether or not the UFO's pose any security threat to the United States, and 3) to determine if UFO's exhibit any advanced technology which the U.S. could utilize.

There is a Blue Book officer stationed at every Air Force base in the nation. He is responsible for investigating all reported sightings and for getting the reports in to Blue Book headquarters at Wright-Patterson Air

Force Base at Dayton, Ohio. The bulk of its investigations, as interpreted by its field officers, has led Blue Book officials to decide that most people do not see extra-terrestrial spacecraft but bright stars, balloons, satellites, comets, fireballs, conventional aircraft, moving clouds, vapor trails, missiles, reflections, mirages, searchlights, birds, kites, spurious radar indications, fireworks, or flares.

On the basis of Blue Book reports, therefore, the Air Force has concluded:

1) No UFO has ever given any indication of threat to the national security.

2) There is no evidence that UFO's represent technological developments or principles beyond present day scientific knowledge.

3) There is no evidence that any UFO's are "extra-terrestrial vehicles."

Neatly arranged evidence and skeptical space scientists to the contrary, many trained observers agree with Donald Keyhoe and the NICAP that the Air Force is not telling all that it knows.

The flying saucer story begins on June 24, 1947 when a young businessman named Kenneth Arnold sighted nine discs near Mt. Rainier in the state of Washington. Arnold described the motion of the unidentified flying objects as looking like "a saucer skipping across the water." In subsequent reports and later sightings, the description was condensed to "flying saucers" and the Boise, Idaho businessman had coined a term that would become known in most languages of the world.

The Air Force immediately denied that they had any such craft and, at the same time, officially debunked Arnold's claim of spotting unidentified flying objects. The civilian pilot had improperly sighted a formation of military planes or a series of weather balloons. Donald H. Menzel, Professor of Astrophysics at Harvard, who was later to become a professional saucer-skeptic and debunker, said that Arnold had been fooled by tilting snow-clouds or dust haze reflecting in the sun.

Arnold, however, stuck fast to his story and the item

made front-page space in newspapers across the nation. For UFOlogists, it was the birth of an era.

The next classic case in the chronicle of UFO sightings was the tragic encounter of Captain Thomas Mantell with a flying saucer over Godman Field Air Base in Kentucky on January 7, 1948.

At 1:15 P.M., the control towers at the base had received a telephone call from the Kentucky State Highway Patrol inquiring about any unusual aircraft which might be being tested in the area. Residents at Marysville, Kentucky had reported seeing an unfamiliar aircraft over their city. Flight Service at Wright-Patterson provided Godman Field with the information that there were no flights of test craft in the area.

Within twenty minutes, Owensboro and Irvington had reported a strange aircraft, which residents described as "circular, about 250 to 300 feet in diameter."

At 1:45 P.M. the tower operators on the base had seen it. They satisfied themselves that it was not an airplane or a weather balloon and called the base operations officer, the base intelligence officer, and several other high-ranking personnel.

At 2:30 P.M., they were still discussing what to do about the object when four F-51's were seen approaching the base from the south. Captain Mantell, the flight leader, started in pursuit of the UFO after the tower asked him to take a closer look at the object in an attempt to identify it.

Mantell was still climbing at 10,000 feet when he made his last radio contact with the tower: "It looks metallic and it's tremendous in size. It's above me and I'm gaining on it. I'm going to 20,000 feet."

Those were Mantell's last words. His wingmen saw him disappear into the stratospheric clouds. A few moments later, Mantell crashed to the earth and was killed. The Air Force issued an official explanation of the incident, which would have been ludicrous had the death of a brave man not been involved. The experienced pilot, they claimed, had "unfortunately been killed while trying to reach the planet Venus."

That was what the officers in the control tower had been watching for all that time—the planet Venus. And that pesky planet was what had lured Captain Mantell to his death. The pilot had thought that he was pursuing something "metallic and tremendous in size" directly above him when, in reality, he was aiming his F-51 at Venus.

As far-fetched as the Air Force's official explanation sounded, it was not without its precedent. During World War II, the battleship *New York,* while headed for the Iwo Jima campaign, sighted a strange object overhead. Officers on the bridge studied it and couldn't make out what it was. It was round, silver-colored, and about the size of a two-story house.

The commander, Rear Admiral Kemp C. Christian, focused his binoculars on the UFO, which seemed to be following the ship. The consensus on the bridge was that it was one of the gigantic balloons that the Japanese had set afloat for the purpose of starting forest fires and bombing cities in the northwestern United States.

The commander called for his gunners to give him the range of the object.

"Seventeen hundred yards," was the answer.

The same order was issued to radar, and the same answer was returned.

"Open fire!" ordered Commander Christian.

The three-inch guns were brought into action, but they couldn't seem to touch the great silver balloon. The *New York's* destroyer escort opened fire with their five-inch guns. Their marksmanship proved to be no better.

About that time, the navigator, who had been awakened by the barrage, came to the deck. Through sleep-fuzzed eyes, he watched the shells zoom up and fall short of their target. He continued to observe the strange action for a few minutes, then, scratching his head sleepily, he walked back to his quarters to make some calculations.

"Sir," he reported to the commander a bit later, "if it were possible to see Venus at this time of the day, you would see it at exactly the same position as the silver balloon."

Commander Christian sputtered, signaled the destroyer escort to have their navigators calculate the position of the planet Venus. The answers, embarrassingly, all came back the same. The battleship *New York* had engaged Venus in combat.

On the evening of July 24, 1948, an Eastern Airlines DC-3 took off on a scheduled flight to Atlanta, Georgia from Houston, Texas. Twenty miles southwest of Montgomery, Alabama, pilots Clarence S. Chiles and John B. Whitted reported a UFO with "two rows of windows from which bright lights glowed." The underside had a "deep blue glow," and a "50-foot trail of orange-red flame shot out the back." Chiles and Whitted were positive that it wasn't the planet Venus that they had seen.

George F. Gorman, a 25-year-old second lieutenant in the North Dakota Air National Guard was waiting his turn to land at Fargo on October 1, 1948 when a bright light made a pass at him. When he called the tower to complain about the errant pilot, he was informed that was no other aircraft in the vicinity except a Piper Cub, which was just landing, and Gorman's own F-51.

Gorman could still see the mysterious light off to one side, so he decided to investigate. Within moments, he found himself in a collision course with the strange light, and he had to take the F-51 into a dive to escape the unswerving globe of light. The UFO repeated the attack, and once again Gorman just managed to escape collision.

When the UFO at last disappeared, pilot Gorman was left shaken and convinced that "its maneuvers were controlled by thought or reason."

After these three "classic cases" in 1948, as well as numerous other less dramatic sightings, many Air Force pilots were reminded of the weird "foo fighters," which several Allied personnel had seen in World War II. Often while on bombing missions, crews noticed strange lights that followed their bombers. Sometimes the "foo's" darted about. Other times they were seen to fly in formation. Several pilots reported seeing the "foo-fighters" during combat.

Barracks and locker-room scuttlebutt had classified

the "foo-fighters" as another of the Nazis' secret weapons, but not a single one of the glowing craft was ever shot down or captured. And, Allied pilots had to agree, if the Germans had come up with another military invention, it was certainly harmless enough—especially when compared to the "buzz-bomb." Outside of startling the wits out of greenhorn pilots, there is no record of a "foo" ever damaging any aircraft or harming any personnel.

The "foo's" were spotted in both the European and Far Eastern theaters, and it came as something of a surprise to thousands of pilots when the Air Force officially decreed that the mysterious lights had never actually existed at all—or were hallucinations at best.

Many Allied pilots, however, had kept quite an account of the "foo's" and had begun to theorize that the things operated under intelligent control. It came as no shock to these pilots when waves of "foo's" were sighted over Sweden in July of 1946.

A kind of hysteria gripped the Scandinavian country, however, and the mysterious "invasion" was reported at great length in all the major European newspapers. Some authorities feared that some new kind of German "V" weapon had been discovered and unleashed on the nation that had remained neutral throughout the duration of World War II. Others tried to explain the unidentified flying objects away as meteors—peculiar meteors that disappeared and reappeared and made an infernal roaring, but meteors nonetheless.

Too many eyewitness reports were appearing in the newspapers to make either theory tenable. If they had been some new kind of V-2 or "buzz bomb," they surely would have caused great destruction in Sweden. Then, too, who would have been launching the bombs? The Nazi war machine had been destroyed, and the Allies were busy dividing Berlin, conducting atrocity trails, and apprehending German scientists for their respective space programs. As for their being meteors, bolides simply do not maneuver in circles, stop and start, or look like metal cigars.

Because of the large-scale interest in the objects which

had been generated in Europe, the London *Daily Mail* sent a reporter, Alexander Clifford, to interview Swedish and Danish military personnel and to conduct an investigation of his own.

Clifford's subsequent report listed certain facts upon which all eye-witnesses to the Swedish "ghost rockets" had agreed: 1) the objects were shaped like cigars; 2) orange or green flames shot out of their tails; 3) they traveled at an altitude of between 300 to 1,000 meters; 4) their speed was about that of an airplane; 5) they made no noise, except, perhaps, a slight whistling.

It may have been an Air Force officer who remembered the "foo fighters" who gave that order on July 26, 1952 to "Shoot them down!" when dozens of UFO's suddenly converged on Washington, D.C.

Several prominent scientists, including Dr. Albert Einstein, protested the order to the White House and urged that the command be rescinded, not only in the name of future inter-galactic peace but also in the name of self-preservation. If Washington was about to host a group of extra-terrestrial space creatures, who had the ability to travel through space, they would certainly look upon an attack by primitive jet firepower as a breach of the universal laws of hospitality.

The "shoot-'em-down" order was withdrawn on White House orders by five o'clock that afternoon. That night, official observers puzzled over the objects both on radar screens and with the naked eye, as the UFO's easily outdistanced Air Force jets, whose pilots were ordered to pursue the objects but to keep their fingers off their triggers.

Although the Air Force was flippantly denying the Washington, D.C. flap within another 24 hours and attributing civilian saucer sightings to the usual causes of hallucinations, planets, and stars, the national wire services had already sent out the word that for a time the Air Force officials had been jittery enough to give a "fire at will" order.

On May 15, 1954, Air Force Chief of Staff General Nathan Twining told his audience at Amarillo, Texas that the "best brains in the Air Force" were trying to solve the problem of the flying saucers. "If they come from Mars," Twining said, "they are so far ahead of us we have nothing to be afraid of."

Somehow, the general's assurance that an ultra-advanced culture would automatically be a benign or an uninterested one did little to calm an increasingly bewildered and alarmed American public. Then, just when important people were beginning to demand that the Air Force end its "policy of secrecy," the much-discussed Air Force Regulation 200-2 was issued to all Air Force personnel.

Briefly, AR 200-2 makes a flat and direct statement that the Air Force is definitely concerned with the reporting of all UFO's "as a possible threat to the security of the United States and its forces, and secondly, to determine technical aspects involved."

Then, in the controversial paragraph 9, the Secretary of the Air Force gave specific instructions that Air Force personnel are not to release reports of UFO's. "Only reports . . . where the object has been definitely identified as a familiar object."

Early in 1959, John Lester of the Newark *Star-Ledger* reported that a group of more than 50 airline pilots, all of them with more than 15 years of experience, had termed the Air Force censorship policies as being "absolutely ridiculous." Each of these pilots had seen at least one UFO, and all had been interrogated by the Air Force. Their consensus was that they were completely disgusted with Air Force procedures and policies.

Lester quoted a pilot as saying that any pilot who failed to maintain secrecy after sighting a UFO was subject to a maximum of 10 years in prison and a fine of $10,000.

"We are ordered to report all UFO sightings," complained a pilot, "but when we do, we are usually treated like incompetents and told to keep quiet.

"This is no fun, especially after many hours of questioning—sometimes all night long. You're tired. You've just come in from a grueling flight, anxious to get home to the wife and kids. But you make your report anyhow and the Air Force tells you that the thing that paced your plane for 15 minutes was a mirage or a bolt of lightning. Nuts to that. Who needs it?"

The commercial pilots have any number of good reasons for being disgusted by the Air Force's making AR 200-2 applicable to them as well as to servicemen. An increasing number of airlines are becoming uneasy about the mysterious air explosions and crashes, which continue to take large numbers of air passengers and crews each year.

Dr. Warren Lovell, a Seattle, Washington pathologist, has investigated more than 150 air crashes involving 2,000 deaths. Last summer, Dr. Lovell was quoted as saying that he could not exclude the possibility of a force "completely unknown to science at present" as the cause of many air crashes.

"I would also not exclude that a force from outer space is responsible," Dr. Lovell said, "no matter how unlikely this possibility appears to be."

The possibility appears less unlikely with each passing month.

Chemists examining the wreck of a Canadian Pacific Air lines DC-6B, in which 52 persons lost their lives, concluded that the plane was destroyed by an explosion which had originated in the toilet, causing the aircraft to split apart. Yet the investigating chemists have found no traces of nitrates that would have been in ample evidence in a conventional explosion. There has been no evidence of bomb injuries, and it has been determined that nobody was in the washroom when the explosion occurred. Was a force "completely unknown to science at present" the cause of the crash?

On February 27, 1960, Vice Admiral Robert Hillenkoetter, U.S.N., Retired, former head of the Central Intelligence Agency, rocked the Air Force when he released to the press photostatic copies of an Air Force directive which warned Air Force Commands to regard the UFO's as "serious business."

The Air Force admitted that it had issued the order

on December 24, 1959, but added that the photostatic copy of the command, which Hillenkoetter had released to the press, was only a part of a seven-page regulation, which had been issued to update similar past orders, and "made no substantive changes in policy."

The official Air Force directive, which was issued to all Air Force Commands on December 24, 1959, indicated the remarkable dual role which the Air Force continues to play in the ever unfolding UFO drama.

"Unidentified flying objects—sometimes treated lightly by the press and referred to as 'flying saucers'—must be rapidly and accurately identified as serious USAF business. . . . As AFR 200-2 points out, the Air Force concern with these sightings is threefold: First of all is the object a threat to the defense of the U.S.? Secondly, does it contribute to technical or scientific knowledge? And then there's the inherent USAF responsibility to explain to the American people through public-information media what is going on in their skies.

"The phenomena or actual objects comprising UFO's will tend to increase, with the public more aware of goings-on in space but still inclined to some apprehension. Technical and defense considerations will continue to exist in this era.

". . . AFR 200-2 outlines necessary orderly, qualified reporting as well as public-information procedures. This is where the base should stand today, with practices judged at least satisfactory by commander and inspector:

"Responsibility for handling UFO's should rest with either intelligence, operations, the Provost Marshal or the Information Officer—in that order of preference, dictated by limits of the base organization;

"A specific officer should be designated as responsible;

"He should have experience in investigative techniques and also, if possible, scientific or technical background;

"He should have authority to obtain the assistance of specialists on the base;

"He should be equipped with binoculars, camera, Geiger counter, magnifying glass and have a source for containers in which to store samples.

"What is required is that every UFO sighting be investigated and reported to the Air Technical Intelligence Center at Wright-Patterson AFB and that explanation to the public be realistic and knowledgeable. Normally that explanation will be made *only* by the OSAF Information Officer. . . ."

Quite a statement for an organization that has repeatedly claimed that 1) UFO's are non-existent; 2) anyone who sees one is suffering from an hallucination or is ignorant of the true natural phenomena (i.e. planets and stars and swamp gas) which he is observing; and 3) even if they do exist they are absolutely unimportant and unworthy of study.

Obviously the Air Force is very much aware of the UFO—aware and actively investigating—in spite of official dismissals.

The Washington, D.C. based National Investigations Committee on Aerial Phenomena accuses the Air Force of doing much more than issuing official disclaimers. NICAP's position is that the Air Force rigorously censors UFO news and suppresses facts that would indicate the saucers to be of extra-terrestrial origin.

NICAP does not seek its members from the lunatic fringe of saucer-watchers. Headed by Donald Keyhoe, a retired Marine Corps major, the Committee welcomed former C.I.A. head R. H. Hillenkoetter to its board of directors. Dewey J. Fournet Jr., a former UFO expert for the Air Force is a member, and so are Dr. Charles P. Oliver, professor emeritus of astronomy, University of Pennsylvania; Albert Chop, a NASA official at Manned Spacecraft Headquarters in Houston; Rear Admiral H. B. Knowles, (U.S.N. Ret.); and J. B. Hartranft Jr., head of the Aircraft Owners and Pilots Association, to name but a few others.

On the one hand, then, there is the NICAP charging the Air Force with censorship and supplying their own 184-page report entitled *The UFO Evidence,* which concludes that the flying saucers are "most likely spaceships" of an extra-terrestrial origin that "appear to be intelligently controlled," and on the other we have Major Hector

Quintanella Jr., head of Project Blue Book, who summarizes the Air Force's position by saying: "There is nothing to indicate that any of these phenomena are extraterrestrial in nature."

Dr. J. Allen Hynek, director of Northwestern University's Dearborn Observatory and former director of Project Blue Book, has gone on record as saying that he believes that there must be something to at least some of the UFO sightings. "The level of intelligence of the observers and reporters of UFO's is certainly at least average and, in many cases, decidedly above average. In some cases, embarrassingly above average."

After the Michigan sightings this March, Dr. Hynek told reporters that "when good solid citizens report something puzzling, I believe we have an obligation to do as good a job as we can. I regard our 'Unidentifieds' as a sort of blot on the escutcheon. Somehow we scientists should be able to come up with answers for these things."

Major Quintanella agreed that it was "impossible to prove that flying saucers do not exist," and that the Air Force should persist in investigating UFO sightings. "We are spending millions to get our spacecraft to the moon and beyond. Imagine what a great help it would be to get our hands on a ship from another planet and examine its power plant."

Although Major Quintanella may have uttered that statement with his tongue wedged firmly in his cheek, the public displays of ostentatious denials to mask the private inquiries and laborious research are becoming much more apparent to even the casual observer.

On April 5, 1966, Dr. Harold Brown told the House Armed Services Committee that there is no evidence to support the claims that the UFO's are spaceships. The formal hearing on UFO's was prompted by the rash of sightings in Michigan in March.

"You might call the study of UFO's a study in puzzlement," Dr. Brown said as he credited the Michigan saucers to "marsh gases."

Dr. Brown concluded by saying: "The Air Force is hiding nothing."

Nothing? When Dr. J. Allen Hynek held his press conference to dismiss the Michigan sightings as will-o'-the-wisps in a swamp, he was honest enough to add this disclaimer: "Scientists in the year 2066 may think us very naive in our denials."

On April 6th, Several persons reported seeing an unidentified flying object three miles south of Iowa City, Iowa. Howard Fountain, who lives in this area, said that he saw a red light slowly descending at an altitude of 2,000 to 3,000 feet. Iowa City police and highway patrolmen said the object appeared to them to be nearly motionless. Mr. and Mrs. Lyle Wilson and their three children observed two bright red lights moving in a circular pattern for about 15 minutes.

On April 7th, a retired army major, Wayne Aho, announced his plans to utilize the Seattle World's Fair 600-foot space needle as a spotting station for UFO's. Aho said that he intended to place two spotters armed with telescopes or binoculars on each side of the tower.

"We would have them on duty night and day," Aho told reporters.

Dr. Hynek was wise in making his present judgment subject to reversal. British author Arthur C. Clarke has given an excellent rule-of-thumb in his book, *Profiles of the Future:* "When a scientist states that something is possible, he is almost certainly right. When he states that something is impossible, he is very probably wrong."